THE GREAT DELIVERANCE

STUDIES IN THE BOOK OF EXODUS

by

Edward R. Dalglish

BROADMAN PRESS
Nashville, Tennessee

4212-14
ISBN: 0-8054-1214-X

Dewey Decimal Classification: 222.12
Subject heading: BIBLE O. T. EXODUS

Library of Congress Catalog Card No. 76-57507
Printed in the United States of America

Preface

The book of Exodus ranks among the most important books of the Old Testament. It is basic for one's understanding of the faith of Israel. Many of its words and thoughts are integrated into the New Testament. It involves two of the paramount events in Israel's history: the exodus from Egypt and the covenant at Sinai. Its themes are varied and refreshing; narrative and law, song and description compose its contents. Exodus is a book to be enjoyed; one rises from its study with larger vistas of life and profounder appreciation of the past. Event and personality unite to implement its moving drama.

The present book is intended to guide the reader in his exploration of Exodus, to point out and discuss frankly some of the critical areas, and to provide an orientation to a Christian interpretation of its themes. It is not intended to be a verse-by-verse commentary. Rather it is designed to assist one in the presentation of Exodus in its ancient setting and in its modern relevance. The materials have been divided into five sections. Chapters II–V are subdivided into three parts; each part is followed by "Theological Reflections," which represent a Christian approach to the particular material under review.

Quotations from Old Testament books come from a variety of translations, including the author's own rendering; most New Testament quotations come from the Revised Standard Version. Others are marked with the abbreviation NEB for *The New English Bible*,

It is a pleasure to acknowledge the kind services of Gary

Klingsporn, who prepared the manuscript for the press, and of the two secretaries who did the typing, Mrs. Kenneth Bohn and Rebecca Sharpless.

I inscribe the book to one though absent was near and dear in the hours of its preparation: *In memoriam Florence Margaret Dalglish.*

E.R.D.

Waco, Texas
1977

Contents

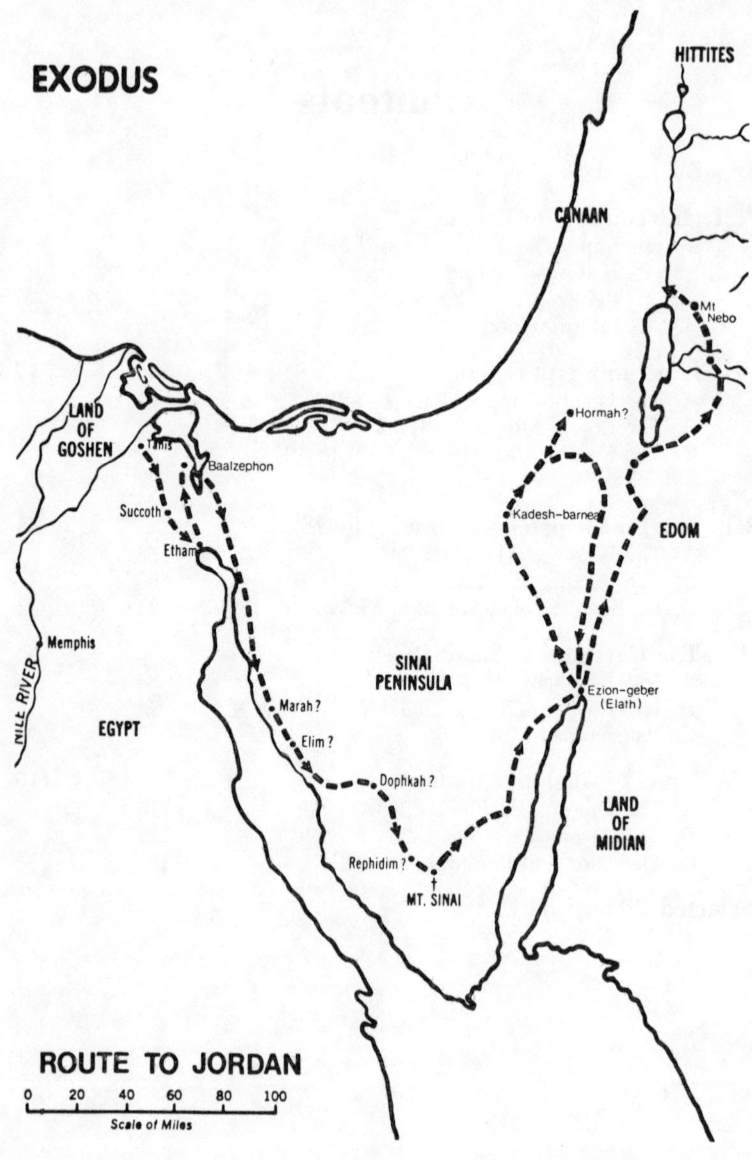

EXODUS
HITTITES
CANAAN
Mt
Nebo
LAND
OF
GOSHEN
Tanis
Baalzephon
Hormah ?
Succoth
Kadesh-barnea
EDOM
Etham
Memphis
NILE RIVER
SINAI
PENINSULA
Ezion-geber
(Elath)
Marah ?
EGYPT
Elim ?
Dophkah ?
LAND
OF
MIDIAN
Rephidim ?
MT. SINAI
ROUTE TO JORDAN
0 20 40 60 80 100
Scale of Miles

I

Introduction to Exodus

A. Its Importance

The book of Exodus is the sequel to Genesis and presents the historical and religious development of the Israelitic nation in its early and critical stages. It provides much of the thought patterns underlying both the Old and New Testaments.

The title Exodus [1] means the "road out." It suggests one of the major themes of the composition. By whatever name this experience may be called, the exodus motif expresses one of the deepest yearning of mankind. Ancients and moderns unite in wanting an "out" (*ex*). Patriots cry for liberty; idealism identifies with the "poor . . . huddled masses yearning to breathe free." Contemporary philosophers seek a way out of meaninglessness and absurdity to the illusive land of authentic being. *Exodus* was the befitting name given to one of the greatest of all motion pictures which portrayed the modern exodus of the Jews. The plight of the underling commands our support. We empathize with the Cinderella. Something within us doesn't love a wall.

The importance of Exodus may be further judged by its pervasive influence on the later books of the Old Testament. One-fifth of Deuteronomy is composed of quotation, amplification, or reference to Exodus. The book of Psalms derives many of its major themes from it; twelve of its compositions are directly based upon incidents described therein. The so-called "Book of Consolation" (Isaiah 40—55) dilates and contemporizes the Exodus motifs. It likens the anticipated deliverance from the Babylonian captivity to a second exodus when deliverance from bondage, passage through the sea, destruction of the foe, a way through the desert, sustenance in the way, and the presence of God in the midst are to be realized again.

It also stresses the call and mission of Israel to the world as does the book of Exodus.

The paramount importance of the book of Exodus for the Christian church lies in the fact that it provides a deeper understanding of the New Testament because quotations and allusions from Exodus are scattered throughout its pages. The themes such as the Passover, the Decalogue, the covenant, the manna, the tabernacle, and the priesthood which are used in the New Testament are funded from the pages of Exodus. Forty-four quotations in the New Testament are from Exodus. These represent twenty-six separate passages in Exodus with one quoted six times, two five times, one three times, and three twice. In addition, out of the 120 references to the Old Testament in the New, 35 references are to Exodus or better than 30 percent.

B. Its Historical Setting

It is generally agreed that Rameses II (1304–1237 B.C.), probably the most significant pharaoh in Egyptian history, was the ruler with whom Moses negotiated. His successor, Merneptah (1236–1223 B.C.) set up a votive tablet in his fifth year, commemorating his victory over his enemies, among whom Israel is mentioned. This is the first historical occurrence of the name Israel in a contemporary document and provides an incontestable date of ca.1231 B.C. for the presence of Israel in the land of Canaan. The way that the name *Israel* is written in the tablet suggests a people rather than a sedentary population and would indicate a certain migratory pattern of Israelitic life as of that period. This accords with all the information we have in Joshua and Judges as well as with the evidence of archaeology. The fact that Israel built for Pharaoh the store cities of Pithom and Raamses in the delta country strengthens the view that Rameses II was the pharaoh of the exodus since in the days of his successor, Israel was in Palestine. That one of the store cities bears the name Raamses tends to exclude any other pharaoh save Rameses II.

The chronological data of this period do not permit anything more than a general dating for the events under review. If we admit that all Israel went down into Egypt, and all participated in the Exodus experience, a view which has vastly more support than other reconstructions, the entry into Egypt of the Israelites and the length of their sojourn can be estimated generally from the following references.

The entrance into Egypt is described in Genesis 46 and summarized in Exodus 1:1–7. The length of their sojourn admits of two views. In Exodus 12:40 f. it is said to be 430 years, but in the Greek and Samaritan versions the 430 years are qualified as the period of time spent both in Palestine and in Egypt. Since the patriarchs sojourned in Palestine some 215 years, it provides an additional 215 years for the sojourn in Egypt (Gen. 12:4; 21:5; 25:26; 47:9; Gal. 3:17). The 430 years are presented in a round figure of 400 years or four generations (Gen. 15:13). This concept of a generation being equal to a century underlies the genealogy in Exodus 6:1 ff. also. Jacob lived 17 years in Egypt (Gen. 47:9,28); his son Levi, 137 years, his grandson Kohath, 133 years while his great grandson, Amram, the father of Aaron and Moses, died at the age of 137. Moses was 80 years old when the exodus occurred. The total period from the descent of Jacob to the Exodus is thus to be figured in terms of four generations. The entire number of years the above named Levites lived, added to the 17 years of Jacob's residence in Egypt, amounts to some 504 years. If we allow 100 years for overlapping of the paternity, a general figure of four centuries is had for the duration of the sojourn. It is not an unreasonable figure and would place the descent of Jacob into Egypt in the era when the Hyksos chieftains dominated the land (1720–1570 B.C.).

Asiatics appear very often in the long course of Egyptian history. In a wall painting in the tomb of Khnumhotep III at Beni Hasan, dating about 1890 B.C., a caravan of Asiatics bringing cosmetic antimony to Egypt is brilliantly portrayed. In the time of Pharaoh Haremheb (ca. 1320 B.C.) there is a report from a frontier official to the effect that Asiatic shepherds had entered the delta area from their famine-swept land, as they had done "after the manner of your fathers' fathers (Haremheb) since the beginning" (cp. Gen. 12:10; 13:1; 26:1; 47:1 ff.). A papyrus list of Egyptian household servants, dating from the mid-eighteenth century B. C., gives the names of the Semitic adults both in Semitic and in Egyptian. These examples could be multiplied to illustrate the intercourse that existed between Egypt and the neighboring countries.

When the Israelites entered Egypt, they were not an inconsiderable group. The household of Abraham had included some 318 "trained men," while he himself was regarded by the Hittite residents in Hebron as a "mighty prince" (Gen. 23:6). Moreover, his flocks were so large that it was necessary for him and his nephew Lot to seek additional pasturelands in order to avoid further domestic clashes between their respective cattlemen. Pharaoh suggested to Joseph that some of the shepherds of Israel might well have the added responsibility of keeping the Egyptian royal herd (Gen. 47:6).

The land of Goshen was no doubt located in the eastern part of the Nile delta. This appears from the fact that it was to serve as the intermediate rendezvous where Joseph journeying from Egypt and Jacob coming down from Canaan were to meet (Gen. 46:28 f.). Goshen was within the territorial boundaries of Egypt (Gen. 45:18; 47:6,11) and afforded the finest pastureland (Gen. 45:18,20; 47:11). The annual inundation of the Nile which occurred from June to October with a mean rise of some twenty-seven feet at Cairo, perennially enriched the delta as it moved toward the Mediterranean through its seven ancient estuaries. In this land of abundance the Israelites continually increased in population and in wealth (Ex. 1:7,12,20; Gen. 47:26).

The Hyksos (Egyptian: "princes of foreign countries") subjugated Egypt from the seventeenth century to the beginning of the sixteenth century. They controlled the delta where they established Avaris as their capital and ultimately went on to dominate the whole of Egypt. The 15th and 16th dynasties belong to them. The conquerors were genuinely abhorred by the Egyptians and are described as living in massive, fortified camps in the delta, scorning the superior Egyptian culture, and primarily interested in the tribute laid upon the conquered. A native reaction commenced in the 17th dynasty when the Theban princes met with some success in engaging the enemy. The task was completed by Ahmose, the founder of the 18th dynasty, who captured their capital at Avaris and liberated the land from the Hyksos yoke.

After the decadent years of the last rulers of the 18th dynasty, Rameses I (1320–1318 B.C.), a native of the northeastern corner of the delta, established the 19th dynasty and had his work carried on by the very energetic rulers that followed him, Sethos I (1318–1304 B.C.) and Rameses II (1304–1237). The actual administration of Egypt was then located in the delta, where Rameses II built Per-Ramesse ("House of Ramesses" Ex. 1:11); and rulers of this dynasty spent most of their time in Memphis or in Per-Ramesse. The continual danger that aliens and nomads dwelling in the delta posed had been painfully demonstrated in the domination of the Hyksos and was so seriously regarded by the rulers of the later 19th dynasty, whose proximity to the alien population magnified the situation, that repressive measures were undertaken. It would appear likely that Sethos I commenced the enslavement of Israel and the infanticide (Ex. 1:8; 2:23) and that Rameses II continued the same policies. The exodus of Israel from Egypt may be placed in the first half of the long reign of Rameses II. When his successor Merneptah (1236–1223 B.C.) succeeded to the throne, Israel was in the land of Canaan.

C. Its Religious Antecedents

Exodus is a chapter, a very important one but only one chapter, in the history of divine salvation. It is the sequel to the descent of Jacob into Egypt and records the very significant events that transpired there. Exodus cannot be understood apart from its antecedents. It must be viewed as part of the continuing development of earlier themes stemming from the patriarchal tradition.

The call of Abram is one of the most important events in world history (Gen. 12:3; see 22:18; 26:4; 28:14). Indeed, it has well been called "the first historical moment." By this is meant that it represents the first moment in history when an individual became conscious of a purpose of universal import: "in thee shall all the nations be blessed." The call is similarly universally oriented. It transcends all particularized culture, soil or ecological milieu, race, ritual, and nature. All of these played no part in his call. He was chosen not because he was a Semite, or a resident in Mesopotamian high culture, or born in a challenge-response of a geographical locale. He was called without priest, without sacrifice, without rite. In a word, his call like his mission transcended all the particularities of his situation; it was a universal call for a universal mission, a call and mission reproducible in the experience of his imitators. To be sure, it was a particular election: God called Abram. But its particularity was purely economic, administrative; it was the subordination of the particular for the universal good. It was the commissioning of one for the blessing of all. There was no favoritism, no chauvinism involved.

The basic promise, then, was the blessing of all mankind through Abram. Three subsidiary assurances were then added: (1) there would be a posterity to effect the blessing (Gen. 12:2; 13:6; 15:4–6; 17:2–6,21; 18:10,14,18; 21:1,2; 22:16 f.; 25:23; 26:4,24; 28:3,14; 35:11; 48:4); (2) there would be protection in order to insure the mission's completion (Gen. 12:3; 27:29; 28:15; and the many deliverances exhibited in the Genesis narratives); and (3) there would be provision and the land (Gen. 12:7; 13:13 f.,17; 15:18–21; 17:8; 24:7; 26:4; 28:4,13; 35:11; 48:4). The major theme, the universal blessing of mankind, was to be implemented by these three subordinate assurances. Again and again in Genesis and Exodus it appears that the divine purpose is going to be thwarted; yet ever and again the mysterious providence obviates the difficulties and moves step by step toward fulfillment. In Exodus the scene may change, the personnel be other; but the same drama, the same themes, the essential purpose are maintained.

D. Its Interpretation

The book of Exodus relates data of the last half of the second millenium B.C. in ancient Semitic thought-forms. Our nurture has been in Graeco-Roman patterns of thought. We must, therefore, adapt our concepts to the ancient Semitic world if ever we are to understand what the book of Exodus is attempting to say.

The book of Exodus resulted from the union of two diverse

sources, one vertical and the other horizontal. The vertical may be conceived of as divine revelation; the horizontal is the inescapable contemporary culture of the Israelites with Sumero-Akkadian roots and other Near Eastern influence. This fusion is frankly acknowledged in the Old Testament. The forebears of the patriarch Abram were confessedly pagan. Abram was essentially the product of Sumero-Akkadian culture. His religion, his language, his thought, his manner of life before his call differed in no great way from his contemporaries. But into his life, as into a lump of dough, came the leaven of divine revelation (Gen. 12:1 ff.). Slowly but surely the leaven began to permeate the lump. The tension between his background in contemporary cultural patterns and the new, divine leaven may be seen in the story of the sacrifice of Isaac. Here the contemporary religious custom, to offer the firstborn, was rejected (Mic. 6:7 f.) and the new ethic of Jahwism discovered. It is no great surprise to see pagan elements in the ongoing history of Israel; it would be most unnatural to have it otherwise. Even after the tutelage at Sinai and in the wilderness, after the conquest of Palestine and its allotment, in his valedictorian address Joshua reminded the Israelites of their pagan antecedents and their contemporary incidence in the national life.

> Thus says Jahweh, the God of Israel, "Your fathers lived of old beyond the Euphrates, Terah, the father of Abraham and of Nahor; and they served other gods . . . now therefore . . . put away the gods which your fathers served beyond the River [Euphrates], and in Egypt, and serve Jahweh" (Josh. 24:2,14 f.; compare vv. 20,23; Gen. 35:2).

The influence of the contemporary cultural background of the Israelites in Egypt may be seen in such stories as the golden calf and its lewd festival (Ex. 32:1–8,19,25), the divine attempt on the life of Moses (Ex. 4:24 ff.), the common Semitic laws taken over by Israel (Ex. 21–23 *passim*), the portable ark not unlike the Egyptian boat-arks (Ex. 25:10–22), and the tent or tabernacle which may be paralleled by pre-Islamic Arabic practice. These and other such narratives, practices, and laws are eloquent evidence of their past. By evaluating the two constituents of Exodus—the contemporary pagan culture inherited by Israel and the dynamic power of Jahwism—we shall be able to interpret this ancient document more correctly. The former is transient; the latter is eternal.

But it is not enough to pinpoint the emergence of Jahwism in its struggle against and transformation of its Semitic cultural inheritance. It is necessary to advance into the interior life of Jahwism, not to view it objectively and externally, but subjectively and empathetically from a point within. Graeco-Roman thought demands logical unity. Israel and the ancient Near East generally affirmed both aspects of the various religious problems even though they were opposed to one another. To illustrate, it would be affirmed that God has ears, but as firmly denied that he has corporeality (Deut. 4: 12,15). Israel maintained that Moses and the elders saw God (Ex. 24:10 f.), but refused to believe that anyone could see the divine (Ex. 33:20,23; cp. v. 11). Here are two examples of Hebrew affirmation and denial; true in one sense, false in another sense. Both necessary affirmations, but no effort to resolve the difficulty is attempted.

This interpretative pattern is congenial to such narratives exemplified in Exodus 32—34. On the one side are the repeated promises of Jahweh to maintain the promises of the covenant he had concluded with Israel and sealed with an oath (Ex. 2:24 f.; 3:6–10,16 f.,19). Jahweh dwelt in their midst (25:4; 29:45 f.), a God full of compassion and pity (Ex. 34:6 f.), who had redeemed his people from Egypt (Ex. 15:13 f.,16) and had sworn an oath that Canaan would be theirs (Ex. 6:8; 13:5,11; 33:1). Yet, on the other side, when the people defected, Jahweh is represented as being so angry that he was willing to abandon the entire nation and build on Moses a new people, even insisting that Moses let him alone that he might consume them in his wrath and affirming that he would not go up with them, no, not for a single moment, lest he should consume them in his anger for their stiff-neckedness (Ex. 33:5). In the dialogue with Moses which follows, Moses persuaded Jahweh that the destruction of Israel which he had suggested was a bad idea and would create a false impression among the nations that he was unable to perform what he had promised. Jahweh rethought the matter and acknowledges the superior wisdom of the suggestion of

Moses.

This divine volatility cannot be harmonized with the qualities of One who knows the end from the beginning and who changes not. What, then, is the narrative attempting to convey? It is a most effective use of anthropomorphism to affirm very dramatically and forcefully that God is purposeful, merciful, faithful, committed to his promises and their fulfillment (these form an integral part of the drama though absent from a particular scene), but that he is disappointed, disturbed, and outraged by such irresponsible behavior on the part of his people. It is an attempt to portray in human analogies what transpires in the Eternal. This cannot be expressed in any other way but in such human terms. Such an interpretation avoids a simplistic literalism, not to say, profanation of the divine; yet does justice to the matter under review.

If the analogy of the leaven and the lump obtains, a further aspect of the problem of interpretation involves the nature of the affirmation. The Bible is in human language and that limitation prevails. The revelation came through men of a particular culture and age; it was transmitted through them as light passing through a stained-glass window. The light, to be sure, passes through, but the glass colors the rays. Revelation passed through the writers, but the revelation assumed the tincture of the writer's personality and background. The book of Exodus is a distillation of the corporate religious thought of Jahwism; it is an apprehension of that revelation and the subsequent verbalization of that revelation in its resultant translucent form.

The Semitic people generally, and Israel included in their number, are possessed of tremendous emotional capacity. The thought of Israel is not expressed in calculated words of a scientific philosopher, but in the poetic, romantic feelings of the soul, in the sensuous image of a creative imagination, in the rapture of an expansive mind and in the dark depression of abysmal grief. What is necessary to say here is this, that overstatement, impressionism, figurative language, and charged emotion abound in the Old Testament (see Ps. 18, for a good example), but if it is exaggeration it is the more credible to the initiate; indeed, it is an effective means of communicating the metaphysical. The words of the Old Testament are vivacious, enthusiastic, dynamic, motivating, capturing; they get their message across to all who will interpret them fairly. Events are scaled to such heights of feeling and convey such an expressiveness that they tower over the turgid dullness of cold rationalism.

The book of Exodus must not be considered primarily a narration of events in a particular time and place. In its composition are narratives, rituals, and law; but these are presented not as particularistic but as universally analogous. To illustrate, the narcissistic pharaoh was a veritable historical reality, but he is presented as an archetype of all such egocentric personalities driven by selfishness to secure his own personal ends, recklessly overriding all deterrents, abandoning every appeal to logic, and progressively destroying himself. He is a vivid portrait in the gallery of the book of Exodus, a warning to all who emulate his pattern of life (cp. 1 Sam. 5:6). Napoleon, Mussolini, Hitler, not to mention some recent Americans, followed his practice and shared his nemesis. The themes of Exodus contain eternal verities, analogies ever contemporary and repeatable. It is not just a story about Hebrew tribes long ago and far away; it is a dramatic word that confronts us in the here and now. Its themes transcend time and place; they are relevant to us, vitally meaningful, supportive, personal, encouraging, admonishing, beckoning all to look, to hear, to understand, and to live. Ask not then for whom the book was written; it was written for you!

NOTES

[1] In Hebrew the name is *shemoth,* "names," derived from the opening words. Alexandrian Jews translated the Hebrew book into Greek in the second century B.C. and entitled it *exodos,* from which we derive Exodus.

II

Israel in Egypt

(1—10)

A. The Israelite Oppression (Ch. 1)

This introductory chapter may be conveniently divided into three sections: (1) the migration of Israel into Egypt (vv. 1–7); (2) the Egyptian corvée (vv. 8–14); and (3) the Egyptian proscription (vv. 15–22).

1. The Migration of Israel into Egypt (vv. 1–7). These verses form a bridge from the past to the future; they summarize the previous notices of Jacob's immediate descendants (Gen. 35:23–26; 46:8,26 f.), indicate the time of the events to be related, and emphasize the populousness of Israel, a theme recurringly appearing in Genesis (17:6; 28:3; 35:11; 46:3; 47:27; 48:8).

2. The Egyptian Corvée (vv. 8–14). After an indefinite period of time, when the founders of the nation were long since dead and the Egyptian indebtedness to the statesmanship of Joseph had faded, a new king arose in Egypt and reversed the benign policy of state in regard to the ever-expanding Hebrew population in the delta. This change may well have occurred in the time of Sethos I, the first significant ruler of the 19th dynasty. The painful memory that Egypt had been dominated for two centuries by the Hyksos, Asiatic invaders, who established themselves as rulers over Egypt, sensitized the succeeding pharaohs to the real and ever-present danger of an Asiatic threat and influenced their state policies accordingly.

The Israelites were not Egyptian citizens; they were sojourners (Heb. *gerim*, a technical term for resident aliens (Ex. 22:21; 23:9), without political rights, personally free though often victims of injustice and oppression. The Israelites had grown in wealth, in number, and in privilege since they entered Egypt. The best of the land was theirs. They were a power to be reckoned with since their loyalty could not be guaranteed in the event of war. Their potential threat grew when the rulers of the 19th dynasty moved their administration to the delta.

It was expedient, therefore, that Egypt adopt a new policy concerning these resident aliens. The resultant legislation assumed the form of an onerous corvée, the exaction of forced labor on Egyptian public works. It involved the drudgery of all types of menial field work, the maintenance of the irrigation system (Deut. 11:11), the production of brick, and the building of two fortress-storehouse cities in the delta: Pithom and Raamses. The city of Raamses (Egyptian: *Per-Ramesse,* "House of Rameses") may be identified either with the great city of Tanis (cp. Ps. 78:12,43; Num. 13:22) or with Qantir, some eleven miles to the south. Its eminence, beauty, and luxury are extolled in Egyptian literature. Pithom (Egyptian: *Pr-Itm,* "House of Atum") may be identified with a site in the Wadi el-Tumilat, Tell-el-Maskhuta, where statues, votive inscriptions, and sphinxes belonging to Rameses II have been recovered.

While the Israelites were not reduced to actual slavery, the heavy demands of the corvée were extremely rigorous. The government delegated the administration of the work to Egyptian taskmasters who superintended the labor-gangs. These taskmasters in turn appointed from the Israelites, officers who were the immediate overseers of the work force (see 5:6,10,13 ff.). It would appear that the Egyptian policy was calculated to break the power of the Israelites, exact free labor from them in government projects in the delta region, and to control effectively the life of an alien population. But despite the intolerable corvée the Israelites continued to multiply ominously. The Egyptian policy had not been entirely successful. Some attempt to control the population growth of the Israelites seemed necessary.

3. The Egyptian Proscription (vv. 15–22). The new policy which the pharaoh formulated was aimed at limiting the Israelite population by enjoining the midwives who assisted the Israelite women in childbirth to do away with all male children upon delivery. But though Egyptian, as the narrative suggests, Shiphrah and

Puah, the two midwives, clandestinely refused to carry out the royal edict. When their evasion was known to the king, they defended themselves by representing the Israelite women as too speedy in their labor ever to effect the king's command. Accordingly, a sterner measure was adopted. This time the edict was addressed to all the Eyptians with delegated authority to liquidate all the newborn children of the Israelites. The surveillance under which the Hebrew women now had to live made it virtually impossible to escape detection, as the story of the birth of Moses demonstrates. This fearful policy of infanticide, tantamount to genocide, forms the sombre backdrop against which the next scenes of the drama are set and poses the questions: Why should this happen to the messianic community? and what is going to happen now?

Its Religious Significance. In the book of Genesis the paramount theme is that Israel was to become the means of universal blessing. Nevertheless, the chosen family experienced one threatening situation after another, but from every cliff-hanging distress came divine deliverance with its lesson deeply impressed upon its subjects. The record of God's saving acts is the theme that continues in Exodus and necessarily determines the complexion of the narrative. It is the burden of the narrative to make crystal clear that Israel would find her fulfilment only in Canaan—and in Jahweh.

It might be well argued that the Israelites were encouraged to sojourn in Egypt by a divine oracle given to the patriarch Jacob (Gen. 46:2 f.) and that part of their tradition envisioned a sojourn there of some four hundred years (Gen. 15:13 ff.). The tribes had been singularly blessed during their long residence in Egypt. It was their home. They possessed the very best pasture land in the fertile delta (Ex. 17:3). Their diet was excellent: meats, fish, breads, grain, figs, grapes, pomegranates, cucumbers, melons, leeks, onions, garlic—they remembered them all too well (Ex. 16:3; Num. 11:5 f.). Though social contact with the native Egyptians was somewhat restrictive (Gen. 43:32; 46:34; Ex. 8:26), the alien Israelites had enjoyed a most cordial interrelationship (cp. Gen. 45:16 ff.; 50:3,7–11; Ex. 11:3; 12:36). Indeed, the commandment to treat aliens equitably derives its force from the exemplary conduct of the Egyptians (Ex. 22:21; 23:9; Lev. 19:34; Deut. 10:19). And that their poorer neighbors might be festively attired for their religious feast, the Egyptians provided the Israelites with appropriate jewelry and clothing (Ex. 3:18–22; 12:35 f.). To be sure, a militant Egyptian nationalism had appeared which viewed all aliens with suspicion and unfortunately had imposed a heavy corvée upon the Israelites, but who could tell whether it would be recalled as quickly as it had been issued. A little time and Israel could demonstrate its peaceful intentions, and all would be well once again. But to leave Egypt where Israel was so richly endowed and to return to Canaan, even if that were possible, was to exchange a manageable situation for one fraught with disaster (Ex. 16:2 f.; 17:3; 14:12; Num. 14:1 ff.; 20:3–5). If earthly blessings were any index of divine approval, Israel could rightly argue that its place was in Egypt. This pragmatic view which surfaced repeatedly was so emotionally charged that its proponents formulated their view of any exodus in the bitterest of words: "Because Jahweh hated us he has brought us forth out of the land of Egypt . . . to destroy us" (Deut. 1:27). Feelings ran extremely high over the issue.

A profounder conviction of the goal of Israel was inherent in the tradition of Israel. Supportive of Israel's role to be of universal blessing was the promise of the land of Canaan. There was the theater of operation, not Egypt. Every migration to Egypt appeared as a wayward course (Gen. 12:10 ff.). Though the tradition included an oracle that Israel would be in a hostile land for four hundred years, it promised that the people would be subsequently delivered (Gen. 15:13 ff.) and assume residence in Canaan. Jacob was reluctant to go into Egypt with his family and went down only after the encouragement of a divine oracle indicated that the residence would be temporary (Gen. 46:2 f.). To dwell in Canaan was so imperative in the mind of Jacob that he enjoined an oath upon Joseph to bury him in Machpelah (Gen. 50:1–14). As thoroughly Egyptianized as Joseph became, he, too, gave testamentary instructions that when Israel left Egypt, his remains were to be conveyed to Palestine (Gen. 50:24 f.; Ex. 13:19; Josh. 24:32).

Israel could never have realized its destiny in Egypt. The kingdom of God required a more heroic mold. Israel was immature, a fledgling and a child, vulnerable; it needed the discipline of experience, the development of moral integrity, and the loyalty to its ideals. There was a real danger that in the syncretism of the delta, where Egyptian and domesticated Canaanite gods dominated popular religion, Israel would lose her identity as the people of Jahweh. The subsequent history of the people in the wilderness clearly indicates how much of the contemporary paganism Israel absorbed (Ex. 32:1 ff.,25; Num. 25; Josh. 24:14). Jahweh must stir his nest; the fledgling must learn to fly (Deut. 32:11). It was the time to call his son out of Egypt (Hos. 13:1). The fledgling adheres to the familiar nest; it is a painful process for the immature when the nest is stirred. In the mysterious providence of God the Egyptian oppression becomes the occasion when Israel severed connections with Egypt to face the long and arduous road to the promised land.

> Then Israel came into Egypt;
> Jacob sojourned in the land of Ham.
> And the LORD made his people very fruitful,
> and made them stronger than their foes.
> He turned their hearts to hate his people,
> to deal craftily with his servants (Ps. 105:23–25).

Theological Reflections (Ex. 1). William L. Shirer prefaced his sobering work *The Rise and Fall of the Third Reich* with a significant quotation from the American philosopher, George Santayana: "Those who do not remember the past are condemned to relive it." In a review of Israel's experiences in the wilderness, the apostle Paul indicated the purpose for which they were recorded: "These events happened as symbols to warn us not to set our desires on evil things" (1 Cor. 10:6, NEB). From a positive point of view the same apostle points out that "all the ancient scriptures were written for our own instruction, in order that through the encouragement they give us we may maintain our hope with fortitude" (Rom. 15:4, NEB). Every age of the church has discovered in the events and characters of the Old Testament analogies to its own situation. These archetypical patterns, distilled to eliminate the extraneous and properly focused to capture the essential, transcend such secondary matters as time and space, and exhibit in startling relevance images with which one can identify. The significant point of all this is: that the book of Exodus is contemporary, relevant, and vital. It is beamed for your reception and its redemptive message is for all who will receive it.

The archetypal pattern in Exodus, chapter 1, may be summarily given. The people of God are not in the Promised Land, but in the land of Egypt. They have resided there for several centuries. Their economic status was excellent: they possessed the best grazing land of the Nile delta, enjoyed the annual renewal of their land through the inundation, held considerable assets in livestock, and had an abundant food supply. As alien residents they were not subject to military service, but were protected by the Egyptian military might. To all intents and purposes they seem to have had it made.

To be sure, they had a religious heritage reaching back to the patriarchs. It was a matter of regret that some Israelites had succumbed to the fascinations of other gods which saturated the delta area, but one could expect this in the circumstances. On the other hand, their leadership and forebears (Jacob, Joseph, Moses) were puristic and traditional, maintaining the ideal that Israel would some day realize her destiny in blessing the world and have as its base of operation the Promised Land. But most of this religious aspiration was discounted by the average Israelite as he concentrated on his own pragmatic interests.

Moreover, even though Israel might have sentimentally yearned for the fulfillment of the patriarch's vision, the hard facts of life militated against such doctrinairism. Canaan was possessed by its own people; and what improvement would Canaan afford over the luxury of Egypt? To uproot a nation after centuries of Egyptian residence, to endure the unspeakable hazards of a migration to Canaan, to face the unavoidable risks of failure, starvation, and war, to begin life all over again as pioneer emigrants in a foreign land when everything was ready at hand in Egypt were insurmountable obstacles for most people.

If they were experiencing for the moment some discriminatory policies of the Egyptian state, if the corvée had recently embittered their lives, and even if the horrendous edict of genocide had been directed against them, it had not always been so; it was abnormal, precipitated by the restlessness of the times. Things could change overnight; another day and perhaps the entire picture would be different! Better by far to be in Egypt where you knew what you had than to be somewhere in the howling wilderness pursuing a utopian dream!

What we discover in all of this is a religious community with nostalgic ideals largely obscured by compromise and by capitulation to the contemporary scene.

The modern church has likewise its vision, its heritage, its heroes, and its aspirations. It would desire nothing more than to become the authentic people of God, but severe difficulties challenge this achievement. We are beset by our modern materialistic attachment (Ex. 16:3; Num. 11:4 f.); Egypt has become for us enchanted ground; [1] we are at ease in Zion (Isa. 32:9,11) despite the rumble of the distant drums. Some of our membership has been seduced by the siren voices of alien gods. America is becoming increasingly steeped in non-Christian thought and practice which have perceptibly seeped into the Christian church. The Abrahams of our day who go out not knowing where (but with whom) they are going are decidedly a rare breed. To rise up, to leave all, and to follow Christ is regarded as fatuous. We have lost the perspective of ultimate priorities; we refuse to acknowledge our Christian responsibility; and we are unwilling to pay the price of discipleship. When all is said and done, we are quite content like the encumbered Israelites in Egypt.

What, then, of the purposes of God? Do they go by the board when his people withdraw? No, not at all. The resources of God are hardly therewith exhausted. In the "Song of Moses" there is a delightful simile which suggests the answer:

> Like an eagle that stirs up its nest,
>   that flutters over its young . . .
> Jahweh alone did lead him (Deut. 32:11).

As the fledgling prefers the security of the nest rather than to venture forth in the untried and unknown, so Israel in self-indulgence and in what it considered to be self-interest fought off any thought of leaving Egypt. But as the wiser dam realizes that fulfillment for the fledgling is not attainable in the nest but in the untried and uncertain beyond, so Jahweh knew that Israel's destiny would never be attained in Egypt and, therefore, stirred up the nest. Momentarily, in the process, the erstwhile solicitous parent seems to have suddenly turned heartless and cruel, using force to oust the young despite his protesting cries. The seeming inhumanity is later discerned as love in its purest form. The stirring of the nest of Israel began with the Egyptian oppression and its increasing demands made upon the people. Life once without care became bitter, but as the external fails, men retreat inwardly; as the physical world crumbles, men enter the realm of the spiritual. The mesmerized nation slowly began to recover its true identity. Deep thought of change floated in their minds; they reconsidered their heritage and the context of their responsibility.

Ultimately, they were prepared to go, to leave the luxury of Egypt for the unknown way to the land of promise. Strange, is it not, that it was persecution that effected the change in attitude and opened the door for fulfillment of self and of the plans of God? It is ever to be remembered that the darkest moment of the cross was the deepest moment of redemption, that Samaria was evangelized because the church was persecuted in Jerusalem (Acts 8:1 ff.), that the imprisonment of Paul, as he, himself, confessed, "has really served to advance the gospel" (Phil. 1:12). The invasion of the Germanic hordes into the Roman Empire must have appeared as an unmitigated tragedy to the Christian church, but it proved to be the most effective way of winning the barbarian for Christ with dividends ever renewed through the centuries. If, then, in the providence of God the Christian church enters into a period of persecution, we should not greet the distress as though it were something strange (1 Pet. 1:6 f.; 2:21 f.; 4:12 ff.). It could be the beginning of the stirring of the nest, the commencement of maturer patterns of life and thought, and our ultimate fulfillment. And in the darkness let this be Exodus persuasion: "All things are yours . . . the world or life or death or the present or the future, all are yours; and you are Christ's and Christ is God's" (1 Cor. 3:21 f.).

B. The Rise of Moses (2—4; 6:2 to 7:7)

The call and commission of Moses are presented in two different renditions: chapters 2—4 and 6:2 to 7:7. The two accounts have in common the appearance of Jahweh to Moses, the notice of the Israelite oppression, the promise of deliverance from the Egyptian yoke, the reiteration that Canaan will be possessed by Israel, the ineptitude of Moses to speak, and the association of Aaron and Moses in the leadership revolt. Subject matter such as the genealogies, difference in style, diction, and some minor details suggests that the second account derives from priestly tradition. It is significant that Exodus 6:2 begins a new section in the Hebrew Bible (6:2 to 9:35) which served as an ancient weekly reading.

1. His Infancy (2:1–10). The genealogical background of the parents of Moses is presented in 6:14–25. Amram had married his father's sister Jochebed and to this union were born three children: Miriam, Aaron, and Moses. Miriam appears to have been a young girl when Moses was born (cp. 2:4,6); Aaron was three years older than Moses (7:7).

The edict of the Egyptian king condemning all newborn infants to death was in full force when Moses was born. To permit their beautiful baby to be wantonly slain was utterly abhorrent, and yet after three months of concealing the child, the parents knew that sooner or later they would be discovered. Accordingly, they devised an ingenious plan.

Egyptian royalty were impeccably groomed and frequently bathed to maintain hygienic and lustral purity. In the very ancient *Pyramid Texts* the king is cleansed in the Field of Rushes following the example of the sun-god Re who there takes a daily purifying morning bath (*Unas Pyramid Texts:* Utterance 253; cp. Ex. 7:15). It appears to have been a common practice to bathe on arising (cp. the *Hymn to Aton*). No doubt observing that the royal family bathed in the Nile, Jochebed secured a papyrus basket, waterproofed it with bitumen, and placed her baby in it near what we may conceive to be the royal bathing pavilion. She stationed Miriam nearby with instructions governing the situation. As was anticipated, one of the daughters of Pharaoh came down to the Nile to bathe with her ladies-in-waiting and espied the basket among the reeds. When it was retrieved by her slave girl, the daughter of Pharaoh discovered the three-month-old baby who immediately won her heart by his pathetic tears. At this emotional juncture Miriam approached the princess to suggest what was going to be an obvious need, the services of a wet nurse, and was bidden to secure one from among the Hebrews. Miriam returned the joyful news to her mother who was then given official charge of the infant, now a protected member of the royal house whose needs were financed by an Egyptian princess!

It is not to be imagined that this daughter of Pharaoh was the crown princess. The Egyptian royal families were prodigious. Rameses II had more than one hundred children! Nor should we conceive Moses, as the motion picture *The Ten Commandments* does, as a crown prince; he was simply a member of a large royal household, an adopted son of one of the royal princesses.

The actual adoption of Moses is indicated in two statements: "she made him her son" and "she named him Moses," which latter is an integral part of the adoption procedure. The name Moses is Egyptian; it appears as a component in such Egyptian names as Thut*mosis* ("Thot has begotten him" or "Born of Thot") and Ra*meses* ("Born of Re"). Since the princess was Egyptian and would not likely be familiar with Hebrew, it appears that a part of the name Moses has disappeared. The explanation of the name given in the text derives from the fact that Mosheh (Moses) has a Hebrew homonym *mashah*, "to draw out." With such scanty details one can but speculate that Moses' mother may have coined a Hebrew term for the child's name which was similar to the Egyptian term in sound but different in sense. As an adopted son of the royal family Moses would have all the rights and preferments of royalty.

The birth and adoption of a proscribed Hebrew child by the royal family who later became the spoiler of the Egyptians and deliverer of his oppressed people illustrates the mysterious ways of Providence.

2. *His Exile to Midian (2:11–22).* The child matured into manhood. Tradition indicates that when Moses was about forty (Acts 7:23), an incident occurred which was to change the entire course of his life. Deep within his heart there must have been an unresolved tension, a conflict between those patriarchal ideals taught him by his mother and the good life amply provided through his generous benefactress. Something restless within his soul must have prompted him to visit his kinsmen in their pathetic plight. Seeing a Hebrew being flogged by an Egyptian taskmaster, Moses interposed in the situation and slew the Egyptian. Precipitously he had crossed his rubicon; there was now no retreat. Though he concealed the corpse in the sand, the report of the incident rapidly spread and ultimately came to the court of Pharaoh. Meanwhile Moses returned the following day to the sector where the Israelites were working. His heart must have been filled with righteous indignation at the degrading oppression unjustifiably imposed upon his people and with anxiety occasioned by the homicide, not to mention the regret that taxed his memory, of Egyptian kindness that had touched his life; he must have lamented that things were as they were. Another altercation was met upon when he arrived amid his kinsmen. This time it was one Israelite beating another. When he attempted to settle the dispute, the one who was in the wrong arrogantly defied his right to interfere and asked menacingly, "Will you murder me as you murdered the Egyptian?" The words sounded the death knell for Moses. There could be no return to Egypt. He was surely under indictment for a most serious crime: a Hebrew had murdered an Egyptian!

Moses chose the most unfrequented trails to make good his escape and ultimately arrived in the distant land of Midian, deep in the awesome wilderness of Sinai. One should pause a moment and empathize with the lonely fugitive as the years gone by passed in review and as he groped for strength to face a most unpromising, bleak future and all for a thankless deed!

And yet in the land of Midian a small event occurred, but an event which would afford him the sanctuary he needed and the solitude in which to mature. A certain shepherd, Jethro by name, had sent his seven daughters to water his flock. Though they had arrived at the well and were filling the troughs, other shepherds came upon the scene and would have occupied the facility had it not been for the wanderer present at the well. Again, indignant at injustice, he drove off the shepherds and enhancing his chivalry, drew water for the girls' flock. When they arrived home earlier than usual, their father Jethro inquired as to the cause. "An Egyptian rescued us . . . drew water . . . and watered the flock!" (Ex. 2:19). Imagine the excitement a good-looking, debonair Egyptian, who had been so chivalrous to them, would have caused in the minds of seven backhills maidens. Immediately upon learning of Moses' kindness to his daughters, Jethro invited Moses to break bread with him. With nowhere to go and knowing no one, Moses abode at the home of Jethro and in the course of time married one of his daughters, Zipporah. The union was blessed with a son whom Moses named Gershom (associated with the Hebrew *ger sham,* "a stranger there"), for he said, "I have been a stranger in a foreign land." Interesting, is it not, that in the wild, barren wilderness of Sinai, the forlorn but future leader of Israel found a refuge and home for some forty years? However, one can enter the mood that must have often been Moses' as he betrayed his inner world in naming his son: "I have been a *stranger* in a *foreign* land." Yet in that stern discipline of Sinai the future deliverer was being prepared for his majestic role.

3. *His Call (2:23 to 4:17; 6:2–30).* There are two accounts of the call of Moses: the primary account in chapters 2:23 to 4:17 is fresh, vivid, vital, logical in its sequence, sensitive in its narration, and one of the finest documents in all the Bible. The other account in chapter 6 is more of a summary, disjointed and fragmentary; and yet it contains two statements of extraordinary value: one concerns the time when the name Jahweh first occurred; the other reechoes the sublime covenantal promise: "I will take you to be My people, and I will be your God" (6:7; cp. 19:5 f.; Jer. 31:32).

The call of Moses is introduced against its somber background. The years of oppression were multiplied. The old king had died; a new king reigned. There was no change in the rights accorded Israel by Egypt, but there was to be a decided change effected by God. He had heard their moaning in their bondage; he remembered his covenant with the patriarchs and would now turn the fortunes of Israel. Notice the four verbs of divine concern in 3:24,25: *heard, remembered, looked upon, took notice of them,* verbs which are interwoven in the sequel.

Picture the scene: Moses, forlorn in heart and broken in purpose, once a member of the royal Egyptian house, now frozen in the abject role of a shepherd in the wastelands of Sinai, pasturing the flock of his father-in-law. Amid the awesome loneliness of the mountains, at Mount Horeb, he had a vision of a burning bush which the fire did not consume.[2] Turning aside to investigate the paradox, he heard in the vision experience his name called twice. "Here am I," he replied. The voice that had uttered his name now enjoined him from drawing nearer. "Do not come closer. Remove your sandals from your feet, [3] for the place on which you stand is holy ground" (Ex. 3:5). The words presaged the divine presence. Since God was holy, all he touched became holy. If, then, the ground were declared holy, it must be that God were present there; and so he was, as the voice continued: "I am the God of your father, the God of Abraham, the God of Isaac, and the God of Jacob" (3:6; 6:2 f.). In mortal fear Moses turned from the spectacle, for to see God was certainly to perish (Ex. 33:20).[4]

There follows the disclosure of the divine purpose to rescue Israel from the Egyptian bondage and to bring it to the Promised Land (vv. 7–9; 6:5–8). But if this good news delighted Moses, the sequel flabbergasted him: "Come, therefore, I will send you to Pharaoh, and you shall free My people, the Israelites from Egypt" (v. 10). Here was the *commission* overwhelming, frightful, unanticipated, impossible. Immediately Moses objected; he was totally inadequate. Far from being released, God merely assured him of his presence and forecast a sign—that one day he would lead his people to this very place (cp. 3:12).

The abysmal diffidence of Moses to assume such responsibility is now articulated in four more objections. The second excuse Moses attempted was to suggest his profound ignorance of God—he did not even know his name! How could he convince his people that he had been commissioned for the task when the purposes of God were so mysteriously hidden? The response to this objection is the occasion of one of the greatest of all religious utterances.

> God said to Moses, I Will Be What I Will Be (Ehyeh-Asher-Ehyeh). Thus shall you say to the Israelites, I Will Be (Ehyeh) sent me to you. And God said further to Moses, Thus shall you speak to the Israelites: The LORD ("He will be") has sent me to you.
>
> This shall be my Name forever,
> This my appellation for all eternity. (Ex. 3:14 f.)

The importance of this passage derives from five considerations.

1. It introduces the name *Jahweh* for the first time. In its parallel, Exodus 6:2, it is stated that God appeared to the patriarchs as El Shaddai (God Almighty), but did not make himself known to them by his name Jahweh. This suggests that where Jahweh appears in earlier narratives, the name is anachronistic, but quite in keeping with the contemporizing of oral tradition.

2. It presents the meaning of the new name. Jahweh may be regarded as the incomplete tense of the third person singular of the verb *hayah* (to be). Translated into our English idiom it assumes the form, "he will be." To render the term by an English present tense ("I am") is misleading, for the notion of the verb *to be* in Hebrew is not static but dynamic; its essence is *becoming* rather than *being*. The term *Jahweh* or "he will be/become," more fully defined in the words, "he will be what he will be," expresses the absolute unrestricted activity of God. What he will be admits of no qualification, is circumscribed by no limitation, is bound by no prescription. It is the assertion of the Absolute: that his will is definitive, will brook no opposition, will overcome all things.

3. The identity of Jahweh, then, with the God of the patriarchs guarantees synonymous relationships and the fulfillment of the promises. This is the reason that in both passages where Jahweh is introduced (chs. 3 and 6), the sequel is devoted to the deliverance from Egypt and the possession of Canaan.

4. The new name Jahweh, so suggestive of the dynamic activity,

is the guaranteed eternal name. And the name is not merely a vocable; in Jeremiah 16:21 the name of Jahweh is tantamount to the divine activity and power. Accordingly, the oracle in verse 15 eternally pledges Jahweh to his program. His purpose will never change; his plans will be fulfilled.

5. Against this background the commission of Moses must be viewed. It is privilege beyond description, but responsibility fearful and demanding. The gravity of his charge is suggested in the fivefold use of the verb "sent" (3:10,12,13,14,15); Moses was the apostle ("one sent") par excellence of the old covenant, and *sent* in this context it becomes predictable that his mission will be of utmost significance. Yet despite the clear announcement that no one may oppose the divine will, so magnificently unfolded in the new name Jahweh, Moses still managed to protest the call with three further objections.

Moses interposed immediately the deterrent that his people might not believe his story. He had had one disastrous experience with them before (Ex. 2:11–15) which had victimized his years. In response Jahweh empowered him to perform three wonders: to transform his rod into a serpent and vice versa, to have his hand encrusted with snowy scales (leprous in KJV) and revert to its normal condition, and to change water into blood. These three signs, Jahweh said, would convince the Israelites of the integrity of his mission (4:1–9).

The fourth objection then appeared: Moses had difficulty in speaking (4:10–12; 6:28). If he were to be the leader of a people, it were essential for him to communicate well. Since he had ever been inept in this talent, he automatically disqualified himself from the task. But, again, Jahweh reassured him by reminding him that the Creator would provide adequacy in this respect. The divine Presence would be with him and enable him to deliver the message.

Finally, with his carefully buttressed opposition crumbling, Moses blurted out in agonized words: "Please, Lord, send someone else." The divine response is so suggestive, so expressive: "Jahweh became angry with Moses." He would provide Aaron to do the speaking. When Moses received the divine oracle, he was to communicate it to Aaron, and Aaron to the people. The felt brevity of this last exchange makes it perfectly clear that the matter was settled: Moses was commissioned without recall. And the sequel suggests that Moses knew further discussion was impossible, and so the newly-appointed leader began preparations for his task.

4. Preparations for Egypt (4:18–26). With this life-changing call now fully affirmed, Moses must face something quite other than tending sheep in the wilderness; he had to return to the place he forsook forty years prior. Securing the blessing of his father-in-law Jethro (4:18) and mindful of what appears to be another oracle that must be fitted into the background of his call (4:19, a summons to return to Egypt), Moses set out with his wife Zipporah and his sons to return to Egypt (4:20). Then follows an additional oracle in which the contour of the coming negotiations with Pharaoh is again forecast (4:21–23; cp. 3:19; 6:13). The miracles were performed, but these were insufficient to secure the release of his people. A firmer measure was needed in which Jahweh will be pitted against pharaonic power. Israel is not a pawn of political manipulation; it is the firstborn son of Jahweh. If Pharaoh did not release him, Jahweh would slay the firstborn son of Pharaoh. It was a stern oracle of the coming conflict, one that anticipated the nemesis of the fatal Passover (4:21–23).

Theological Reflections

1. *The birth of Moses.* Like Jesus, Moses was born in a most turbulent era when the state had proscribed the newborn. His preservation like that of Jesus was due to the courage of parents who refused to comply with the barbarous edict and sought and found deliverance for the child. "By faith Moses, when he was born, was hid for three months by his parents, because they saw that the child was beautiful; and they were not afraid of the king's edict" (Heb. 11:23). That an infant, under sentence of death by a state, should be rescued, adopted, and educated by an integral part of the same state exhibited for the faithful the unbelievable grace of Jahweh; and to climax it all, his own mother was paid wages for bringing up her own son! It does not always obtain, but it occurs frequently enough to be

significant that behind the great saints of God stand the Jochebeds, the Hannahs, and the Marys with ministering concern.

The early church cherished the final words of its first martyr Stephen, who in Acts 7 recounted the biblical story of the early life of Moses with traditional additions (italicized):

But as the time of the promise drew near, which God had granted to Abraham, the people grew and multiplied in Egypt till there arose over Egypt another king who had not known Joseph. *He dealt craftily with our race and forced our fathers to expose their infants, that they might not be kept alive.* At this time Moses was born, and was beautiful before God. And he was brought up for three months in his father's house; and when he was exposed, Pharaoh's daughter adopted him, and brought him up as her own son. *And Moses was instructed in all the wisdom of the Egyptians, and he was mighty in his words and deeds.*

When he was *forty years* old, it came into his heart to visit his brethren, the sons of Israel. And seeing one of them being wronged, he defended the oppressed man and avenged him by striking the Egyptian. *He supposed that his brethren understood that God was giving them deliverance by his hand, but they did not understand.* And on the following day he appeared to them as they were quarreling and would have reconciled them, saying, Men, you are brethren, why do you wrong each other? But the man who was wronging his neighbor thrust him aside, saying, Who made you a ruler and a judge over us? Do you want to kill me as you killed the Egyptian yesterday? At this retort Moses fled, and became an exile in the land of Midian, where he became the father of two sons (Acts 7:17–29).

2. *The call of Moses* (2:23 to 4:17). In the narratives which describe the call of God to his servants there is a recurrent pattern. One may analyze such call narratives and discover that these experiences of Gideon (Judg. 6:11–36), Isaiah (Isa. 6), Jeremiah (Jer. 1), Amos (Amos 3:8; 7:1–9,14 f.; 8:1 to 9:4), Ezekiel (Ezek. 1—3), and others have common structural similarities. Despite individual particularities these themes persist: the divine confrontation, the introductory word, the commission, the objection, and the reassurance. Some themes are occasionally abbreviated while others are dilated. In the call narrative of Moses all the themes are present; a few are not only reiterated but also developed at some length.

It is quite important to adjust our western mentality to that of the ancient Near East if we are ever to translate their thought idiom into our patterns of understanding. The New Testament states a paradox which if kept in mind will be most helpful in comprehending the nature and meaning of the most important call narrative in the Old Testament—that of Moses. It states that Moses endured "as seeing him who is invisible" (Heb. 11:27; cp. Matt. 5:8). It denies that Moses saw God in any physical manner—that was not possible or significant—but strongly affirms that Moses understood the meaning of God. Most readers would not press for the literal understanding of Isaiah 6, but would rightly interpret it to be visionary. When one is speaking of religious truths, metaphysical entities beyond the control of our senses, he must speak symbolically or analogically. We communicate with one another in anthropomorphic terms, in human terms; we say that God is near us, has spoken to us, has saved us. All these are subjective and metaphysical, expressed in the language of analogy because we cannot do otherwise. The whole point of this argument is to suggest that it was not otherwise with Moses.

Jahweh was preparing his servant for the day of his call. There were mounting tensions deep in the soul of Moses for the welfare of his people and for the accomplishment of that universal purpose of Jahweh. For forty years Moses had vainly suppressed the vision, fought it, rationalized his situation, accused and excused himself. But now this was no longer possible; he must face the moment of truth or self-destruct. The traumatic, psychological upheavals erupting within his inner life and calling for resolution are magnificently portrayed in the call narrative. His resentments, defeatism, and pessimism powerfully color the narrative with his repeated objections to the divine call. And yet as confidence gradually overcame his dark forebodings, he rose to his full stature in this vision of God and assumed the privileged role with unabating conviction and strength. Accordingly, it may be said that the spirit gives life to the narrative, but the letter kills. One might expect to find some clues for the interpreter and he does in that the opening words of the narrative plainly state: "an angel of Jahweh appeared to him." It was a vision within his soul like Isaiah's; the externalities of the vision are to be accordingly interpreted. Six times the term *vision* appears in

Exodus (3:2,16,18; 4:1,5; 5:3). The narrative is the objectifying of what was going on within; it is the external form in which the subjective became conscious.

One might interpose the question here: Did not Jahweh impress with a heavy hand an unwilling Moses into his service? The call to service often finds an immediate response among the shallow, the precipitous, the restless (cp. Luke 9:57–62). These do not have the depth, the determination, the dedication; they cannot endure the trials, the discouragements, the self-giving demands beyond duty. Part of the evangel of Genesis is the deliberate choice of the patriarchs, for their lives were exemplary for and as the people of God. Not that they had arrived, but they felt and responded to that divine attraction that led them from the commonplace to be princes with God. Moses had his problems, deeply seated and aged in disappointment; it was not that he refused. He simply could not believe that now after decades in the howling wilderness, with patterns of life largely dictated, he could undertake successfully a mission whose difficulties he of all men could appreciate. But as the bitter chill of negativism dissipated before the warm, positive, line-for-line encounter with God, he did what alone sufficed: "Here am I; send me!"

> By faith Moses, when he was grown up, refused to be called the son of Pharaoh's daughter, choosing rather to share ill-treatment with the people of God than to enjoy the fleeting pleasures of sin. He considered abuse suffered for the Christ greater wealth than the treasures of Egypt, for he looked to the reward (Heb. 11:24–26).

The choice of God was the choicest of men, and that unsurpassed and without regret, from the mud-pits of Egypt to Mount Nebo's requiem.

The other concern that may be profitably discussed has to do with the nature of the narrative. If one views it with unrelieved literalism, the question then arises why did God the Omniscient become angry with Moses, seeing that he knew the end from the beginning. To respond to this problem one must remember that in matters that concern God our language must be accommodated. Otherwise the unchangeable and unchanging God could become inexorable fatalism in which all the glories of the divine understanding of men would be lost. It would seem fair to consider the call narrative as a whole as an externalizing of the deep psychological upheavals in the religious experience of Moses as he fought with God and with himself regarding that mission of liberation which haunted him for years. The translation of that inner experience, similar to the wrestling of Jacob in a dream experience (Gen. 32:24–32), into the external idiom of literature conveys sensitively vistas of spiritual truth perceptible in no other way. And the dialogue effectively communicates to us the understanding, concern, and empathy of the divine as mortals wrestle with their problems in ultimate identity and proximate resolution.

The call of Moses was preeminently a call to be a prophet. If we may borrow from other books in the Old Testament, the picture so gained presents the prophet as one who has had a life-transforming experience with God. He had stood in the council of Jahweh, had heard his counsel, and was dynamically motivated to proclaim that divine word. His message derived from above, the vertical, from God; it was not from beneath, the horizontal, from man. The prophet was a moral individual, the embodiment of his message, and refused to compromise at any cost. It became a message of woe to a sinful people, to warn them of their disastrous course, and to persuade them of the old and faithful paths.

While the office of the prophet is exhilarating and inspiring, it involves often serious antagonism, hatreds, persecutions, misunderstandings, imprisonment, and at times death (cp. Jer. 1:18–19; Amos 7:10–17).[4] People are estranged from him; society abandons him because of his dark views (Ex. 5:22 f.); he is frequently alone (1 Kings 19:10). At times he cannot understand the ways of God; he feels forsaken, standing in the breach alone against the foe and without the felt support of God with him (Ex. 5:21). Discouragement, loneliness, renunciation of the prophetic office entirely, even death-wishes are not foreign to the consecrated spokesman of God. But despite all of this, Moses exclaimed with genuine passion the glory of the calling: "Would that all Jahweh's people were prophets, that Jahweh would put his spirit upon them!" (Num. 11:29).

There is a divine oracle in Numbers 12:6 to the effect that "if there is a prophet among you, I, Jahweh, make myself known to him in a vision, I speak with him in a dream." Visions and dreams were the normal means of communicating the divine word to the prophet. Joel envisaged a day when Jahweh would pour out his Spirit on all flesh, with the result that sons and daughters would prophesy, old men would dream dreams, young men shall see visions. Even upon the menservants and maidservants (slaves) in those days Jahweh would pour out his spirit (Joel 2:28 f.).

The Christian faith affirms that on the day of Pentecost that prophecy was fulfilled: that all flesh whether young or old, men or women, free or bond, now may have the experience once vouchsafed but to prophets. Dream and vision are tantamount to the knowledge of God; the Spirit is the dynamic empowering agent to bring to fruition the knowledge of God in word and walk. Accordingly, the Christian is numbered among the prophets, the vision and dream of revelation are his, and the Holy Spirit the power to actualize the counsel of God.

It remains to mention one further matter, the meaning of the burning bush. The former quotation from Stephen's speech is continued in a description of the call vision of Moses:

> Now when forty years had passed, an angel appeared to him in the wilderness of Mount Sinai, in a flame of fire in a bush. When Moses saw it he wondered at the sight; and as he drew near to look, the voice of the Lord came, 'I am the God of your fathers, the God of Abraham and of Isaac and of Jacob.' And Moses trembled and did not dare to look. And the Lord said to him, 'Take off the shoes from your feet, for the place where you are standing is holy ground. I have surely seen the ill-treatment of my people that are in Egypt and heard their groaning, and I have come down to deliver them. And now come, I will send you to Egypt.' This Moses whom they refused, saying, 'Who made you a ruler and a judge?' God sent as both ruler and deliverer by the hand of the angel that appeared to him in the bush (Acts 7:30–35).

Above the entrance of the Jewish Theological Seminary in New York City there is an inscription portraying the burning bush with the Hebrew words beneath it ". . . and the bush was not consumed." It is the persuasion that as long as God is in the midst of his people, they are immortal. This is certainly true and one possible view of the emblem. On the other hand, one may view the burning bush in the lonely wastes of the mountains of Sinai as the sign that God deigns to grace the lowly, appears in the commonplace of life, and brings in the desert new hope for the disconsolate of the waste lands.

Yet, true as all this may be, the important focus is the fire rather than the bush. It is the symbol well suited to convey reaches of the divine nature. Fire is ethereal, mysterious, immaterial, illuminating, useful, warming, but irresistible, dangerous, to be handled with care, everywhere producible. But it was not the fire that spoke; it was the voice that spoke *in* the fire. Fire was the insignia, the sensuous externality wherein the divine was present.

Enough has been said of the divine oracle that Moses received there. It remains to point out the singular, yea, stunning beauty of one aspect of the words. Jesus had been confronted by the Sadducees who did not believe in a resurrection. They produced the hackneyed problem that had reduced their opponents by its *argumentum ad absurdum* (an argument that leads to absurd conclusions). It was the case of seven brothers who had honored the law of the Levirate and had in turn married the widow of the eldest brother. The words of the New Testament are unimprovable.

"After them all, the woman died. In the resurrection, therefore, to which of the seven will she be wife? For they all had her."

But Jesus answered them, "You are wrong, because you know neither the scriptures nor the power of God. For in the resurrection they neither marry nor are given in marriage, but are like angels in heaven. And as for the resurrection of the dead, have you not read what was said to you by God, 'I am the God of Abraham, and the God of Isaac, and the God of Jacob'? He is not God of the dead, but of the living" (Matt. 22:27–33).

Three magnificent truths are here enunciated. (1) The ultimate relationship of man is God: "all live unto him." (2) Man is essentially and ultimately an individual. Abraham, Isaac, and Jacob—not the sons of Abraham or Hebrews—are individually related to God. Predicates such as blood, color, race, parents, and sex are secondary and evanescent. (3) The eternal contemporaneity of the divine relationship expressed in the verb "I am" guarantees an eternal connection with God despite the accident of death.

What an ever enlarging sphere we enter when this word of the Lord grips our hearts, "He is not God of the dead, but of the living, for all live unto him" (Luke 20:38, RSV). There are no cenotaphs for his plans, no tombs for his purposes. God deals in life. It is the good will of him that dwelt in the bush (Deut. 33:16).

C. The Contest with Pharaoh (4:27 to 6:1; 7:8 to 10:20)

The narrative commences with the rendezvous of Moses and Aaron at Mount Horeb and the program to which now both were committed. Upon entrance into Egypt the two brothers presented their plans to the elders and to the people and exhibited the authenticating signs. The people were profoundly moved and gave their immediate approval.[5] With the support of the people, Aaron and Moses proceeded to secure an audience with Pharaoh and to petition that the Israelites be permitted to celebrate a festival to their God some three days' journey in the wilderness lest they be visited with pestilence or sword. Despite the marvels performed by Moses before the king, [6] the request was scornfully rejected. Immediate steps were instituted to augment the corvée of the Israelites; henceforth they were to receive no straw from government issuance for their bricks. They would have to provide it on their own and still be responsible for the same quotas.

The momentary success of Moses had been rudely eclipsed. When the Hebrew foremen could not fulfill their quotas, they were beaten. When they appealed their case to the royal court, they received no easement, but rather were maligned as shirkers. The harshness of the royal measures ruptured the relationship between Moses and the people. Indeed, Moses himself rued the situation as lamentably inexplicable. "O Jahweh, why hast thou done evil to this people? Why didst thou ever send me? For since I came to Pharaoh to speak in thy name, he has done evil to this people, and thou hast not delivered thy people at all" (Ex. 5:22 f.).

This chapter has two aspects that call for comment. The first is that the narrative elaborates the impossibility of an Israelite release. If political expediency dictated the policy of oppression, that oppression was intensified by what may have appeared to the king as arrogance on the part of the subjugated in requesting at least a week's vacation or more in order to hold a religious festival! The relations between the crown and the Israelites were at an all time low. More serious, however, was the bitter alienation that developed between Israel and Moses, as voiced by the chastened Hebrew gang-masters. They decried his mismanagement of their affairs and repudiated his mission with imprecation (5:19–21). With every phase of the situation worsening, it would take a stupendous miracle to effect a deliverance. The narrative builds up the problem so that the redemptive power of Jahweh will be the more glorious in the deliverance.

The other aspect has to do with the actual design of Moses. In some passages the total liberation of the people is clearly in view (3:7–10; 11; 12; 6:1,6–8,10 f.,13,26 f.; 7:2,5; 9:28), while elsewhere the request is to celebrate a feast to Jahweh in the wilderness, some three days' journey from the land of Goshen (3:18; 4:23; 5:1–3,17; 7:16,26; 8:4,16,21–25; 9:1 f., 13; 10:3 f., 8–10,20,24–26). Was the plan to be three days' journey from Goshen a specious request to initiate complete escape? More baldly stated, did Moses purposely practice deception in his negotiations with Pharaoh?

The matter becomes clearer when one remembers that the Israelites were resident aliens (Heb. *gerim*). As such they had been admitted to Egypt and dwelt in the land of Goshen. They were without those political rights normally enjoyed by nationalists; nevertheless, they had rights and responsibilities. They were subject to taxes, corvée, and the law of the land, but they were essentially freemen with liberty of movement or emigration. Israel recognized that as long as it chose to reside in Egypt, it would be subject to restrictions, but the crucial problem had now become the unlawful restriction of their freedom of movement. The request to hold religious celebration in the wilderness was within their inalienable rights as *gerim.* If the crown admitted that, it followed that a peaceful withdrawal from Egypt could be effected without difficulty. If, on the other hand, the court refused freedom of movement, it would immediately clarify Egyptian intent at the highest level and make public that the invested rights of a resident alien population were being violated. It was a test case that would force the pharaonic court to define the political status of Israel. The sequel clearly shows that Pharaoh denied Israel's right to freedom of movement and was pursuing a course which would lead to complete enslavement.

To appreciate the tensions within the momentous situation under review some orientation to the significance of the office and role of a pharaoh is desirable. The word pharaoh (Egyptian: *per*^{c}*o*) means "great house." It referred at first to the palace, but came in time to mean its master, much in the same way "Sublime Porte" became identified with the government of the Ottoman sultan. The Egyptian pharaoh was not unlike the emperors of Japan. Bearing the title ("son of heaven") the Japanese emperors were venerated as direct descendants of the sun goddess Amaterasu, who in the fourth century A.D. commissioned her son, the first tenno or mikado, to rule the country of Japan. Even today millions of Japanese recognize Emperor Hirohito as the lineal descendant of the sun goddess and consequently as "an incarnate supernatural being." [7]

Pharaoh was born into the family of the gods. As "lord of diadems" he possessed universal dominion whether political or natural. Every ruler was his vassal; everyone who revolted ultimately perished. He dispensed life and death; nature owned his sway whether it be the inundation of the Nile, the rainfall in the Hittite country, or the Syrian snow. As perfect god his power was immeasurable, his knowledge all encompassing, his dominion unbounding. The monarch's strength was irresistible and no foe could withstand his personal onslaught. Flame from the uraeus (sacral serpent on his head gear) destroyed his foes. Everything which he ordained came about. His protocol, insignia, cult, and regal activity proclaimed his divinity, which in turn, buttressed the cosmic dimensions of life and death. It is with this absolutism and grandiose mythological background of the Egyptian crown that the narratives depicting the contest with Pharaoh must be interpreted.

The relations between Egypt and Israel had other aspects equally disruptive. The Egyptians considered themselves the favored of the gods, for what land had such a salubrious climate, what nation was so amply provided for by the inundation of the Nile which perennially revitalized the land and whose flanks were protected from outside foes by the forbidding deserts? In art and architecture, in economic wealth and sophisticated culture, in international prestige and domestic abundance the Egyptians outstripped their neighbors by a wide margin. They were the privileged, the favored of the gods, confident in life, sophisticated, optimistic. However, when they compared themselves thus with others, their higher privileges gave rise to national arrogance. They considered themselves to be "the people"; all others were barbarians.[8] This felt superiority is nowhere more pronounced than when they compared themselves with the Asiatics.

> Lo, the wretched Asiatic, unpleasant is the place where he is, (with) trouble from water, difficulty from many trees, and the roads thereof awkward by reason of mountains. He does not dwell in one place, being driven hither and yon through want, going about (the desert) on foot. He has been fighting since the time of Horus [i.e. for ever]; he never conquers, yet he is not conquered, and he will not announce the day of combat, like a thief whom a community has driven out.
>
> *The Teaching for Merikare,* 91 f.

Such an arrogant posture contributed to the alienation between the Egyptians and the resident aliens. It precluded any sympathetic understanding of the minority group and any enlightened efforts to improve their situation. But Winston Churchill reminded the world that "if a Government has no moral scruples, it often seems to gain great advantages and liberties of action, but 'All comes out even at the end of the day, and all will come out yet more even when all the days are ended.' "[9]

The Egyptian Plagues (7:14 to 10:29). There are nine plagues described in this narrative: 1. pollution of the Nile (7:14–24); 2. frogs (7:25 to 8:15); 3. gnats (8:16–19); 4. insects (8:20–32); 5. pestilence among cattle (9:1–7); 6. boils (9:8–12); 7. hail (9:13–35); 8. locusts (10:1–20); and 9. darkness (10:21–29). Though the space allotted to them varies from four to twenty-three verses, a persistent literary pattern is observable with the following five themes generally present: (1) introduction, in which occurs the request for release and/or the announcement of the plague; (2) the plague itself; (3) the response of Pharaoh or a notice of the magicians; (4) the removal or endurance of the plague; and (5) the persistent obduracy of Pharaoh.

The plagues may be explained as a series of natural disasters which befell Egypt during a particular period commencing in June and continuing through the following April. Apparently, shortly before the inundation, in the month of June, when the Nile is at its lowest level, the river became putrid with its water impotable and of reddish cast (cp. 2 Kings 3:22 f.).[10] Frogs multiplied prolifically in the shallow waters of the river system and then as quickly perished. The conditions were exceedingly favorable for the emergence of insects in the silt of the receding Nile. Gnats and mosquitoes followed spreading disease among cattle and men. In the delta, drops in temperature and rainstorms occurred between the end of November and the end of March with roads almost impassable at times. The hailstorm ruined the winter cultivation which was normally harvested in May in the delta region. Locusts from the Libyan desert, blown in by a southwest wind, next ravaged the stricken area; and finally the sandstorm (*Chamsin*), arising generally in the south, darkened the land with its dust and halted all activity. All these phenomena have been witnessed in Egypt within recent history. As individual natural events they cannot be viewed as uniquely preternatural. The miraculous element lies rather in their concentration in time and their forecast by Moses. Plague followed plague, repeatedly, relentlessly, and with such intensity that the Egyptians were fully convinced that the signs, miracles, and wonders were the work of Jahweh. This is the only adequate explanation for their release of Israel.

The narratives are essentially a theological interpretation of the startling event. In the ancient Near East it was a common belief that behind the visible earthly scene was the controlling world of the gods. Mortals were mere pawns in their hands. Each nation had its own gods who sponsored and supported both king and subject. The Mesopotamian rulers, however exalted they might be, owned the sway of the gods, ruled the land as vicars, fought as divinely commissioned, and honored the true potentates above. In the following narrative of one of the campaigns of Hammurabi the role of the monarch is typical.

> (Encouraged) by an oracle (given) by Anu and Enlil who are advancing in front of his army, (and) through the mighty power which the great gods had given to him, he [Hammurabi] was a match for the army of Emutbal and its king Rim-Sin.

More than a millennium later the same concept of war as a conflict of the divine world is seen when Rabshakeh, the military envoy of Sennacherib, challenged Hezekiah to open combat with his troops, sarcastically affirming that the Judean king had done injury to his God Jahweh in the demolition of altars and high places and that, contrary to the opinion of Hezekiah, Jahweh had instructed the Assyrians to wreak vengeance upon the Judeans for this impiety (2 Kings 19:19–36; Isa. 36–37).

Israel waged war in the name of Jahweh. With strict observance of its holy character and with the ark of the covenant leading the army, the Israelitic host advanced to the fray (1 Sam. 4:3 ff.; 2 Sam. 11:11). The power, direction, victory, and spoils belonged to Jahweh (see Josh. 5:13 ff.; 7:2 ff.; 1 Sam. 6:5 f.; Ps. 44:4 ff.). Even the stars fought in their battle order from heaven against Sisera (Judg. 5:20).

The conflict with Pharaoh was not dissimilar. Against all the gods of Egypt Jahweh executed judgments (12:12). By signs, wonders, and marvels (4:8–9,17,21,28,30; 7:3,9; 8:23; 10:1 f.; 11:9–10; Ps. 78:42; 135:9; Jer. 32:20 f.), with a strong hand and outstretched arm (6:1,6), with great acts of judgment and with a greater power (6:6; 6:1), Jahweh manifested himself as the unique and omnipotent God, who controlled the forces of nature and the flow of history. And the irony of the situation was that Jahweh displayed his irresistible power in the proud land of Egypt where the divine pharaoh was all powerful.[11] The struggle is portrayed in the Song of Miriam in a wealth of vocabulary stemming from warfare: enemy, adversaries, overthrow, destroy, spoil, war, chariots, army, and picked officers (Ex. 15). Jahweh fought for Israel (14:25)

> Jahweh is a man of war;
> Jahweh is his name.

Pharaoh's chariots and his host
he cast into the sea
(Ex. 15:3 f.).

The struggle with Pharaoh was not arbitrary; its purpose was both revelatory and redemptive. These aspects are remarkably presented in two significant passages: Exodus 9:14–16; 6.

The first passage asserts that the plagues were visited upon a pagan ruler and his nation in order that they might know God (cp. 2 Chron. 33:13).

This time I will send all my plagues upon your person, and your courtiers, and your people, *in order that you may know that there is none like me in all the world* (compare 8:6). I could have stretched forth my hand and stricken you and your people with pestilence, and you would have been effaced from the earth. Nevertheless I have spared you for this purpose: *in order to show you my power*, and *in order that my fame may resound throughout the world* (Ex. 9:14–16; the italics are the writer's).

Elsewhere in the narrative of the struggle similar objectives are present:

. . . that you may know that I am Jahweh (7:3,17; 8:18; 14,4,18)
. . . that you may know that the earth is Jahweh's (9:29);
. . . that you may know that Jahweh makes a distinction between Egypt and Israel (8:19; 9:4,26; 10:23; 11:6)

The manifestation of Jahweh confronted the Egyptian magicians with their specious wonders (7:11,22; 8:3), vanquished them ignominiously (8:14; 9:11), and drew from them the confession: "This is the finger of God" (8:19). The Egyptian courtiers were initially as obstinate as Pharaoh, but with the successive plagues some of them commenced to respect the word of Moses (9:20). Ultimately, they turned on Pharaoh and censured his policy. "How long shall this one [Moses] be a snare to us? Let the men go to worship Jahweh their God! Are you not aware that Egypt is lost?" (10:16). Nevertheless, the king persisted in his inexorable stance through three more plagues until he was forced to release Israel. The plagues provided Jahweh a means whereby he could make himself known, a display of his sovereignty over nature and history.

That he made a distinction between Egypt and Israel (8:18 f.;

9:4,26; 10:23; 11:7) was hardly favoritism; rather it was an affirmation that the God who had manifested himself in the marvels and wonders of the plagues, identified with his chosen people Israel through whom his universal purpose would be wrought. If Pharaoh were convinced of the uniqueness and sovereignty of Jahweh, the only adequate response would have been similar to that of Emperor Hirohito of Japan, a frank and public disavowal of the false pretensions wherewith his office was invested. Were it not possible that Egypt might then have become a people of Jahweh, too, as a later prophet envisioned (Isa. 19:24) if a nobler character had occupied the throne?

Another aspect of the revelation of Jahweh in the contest with Pharaoh was the demonstration of his long-suffering and forbearance with a most obdurate ruler till there was no recourse but judgment. It is generally agreed that the principles of the natural and spiritual world cannot be broken with impunity. One may violate the moral confrontation until evil becomes good, bitter becomes sweet, and darkness light (Isa. 5:20). What the modern might term moral law would be spoken of as more personally involving God in ancient Israel. Pharaoh is said to have hardened his heart, that is, to have rendered himself unimpressionable (8:11,28; 9:34; 10:1). Pharaoh's heart is described also as being hard, obdurate (7:13 f.,22; 8:15; 9:7,35). Again, Jahweh is said to have hardened Pharaoh's heart (4:21; 7:3; 9:12; 10:20,27; 11:10; 14:4,8,17). Pharaoh was free to choose, to act, capable of self-determination, but his mind and will were intransigently committed to his own selfish ends. The Hebrews affirmed paradoxically both free will and divine predeterminism. Man is capable of self-determination; otherwise he is not made in the image of God. God is in control of all; otherwise he ceases to be God. Both truths are here affirmed in the case of Pharaoh. He willfully hardened his heart and retributively Jahweh hardened Pharaoh's heart—one process, two aspects.

But let us not lose sight of its significance in the context. Jahweh dealt patiently, sympathetically, and kindly with the haughty king through a period of some nine months, removing the plague at the slightest suggestion of repentance moderating the intensity of the damage, and that through nine different occasions! The mercy of Jahweh was singularly displayed in his dealings with Pharaoh and Egypt.[12] The revelation of Jahweh's judgmental righteousness appeared at that point where to indulge the ruler further would have been culpable.

The dynamic righteousness, ultimately manifest in the plague of the firstborn, became for Israel the high redemptive moment when its days of being downtrodden and tormented were over. It was a singular declaration that Jahweh was the vindicator of the oppressed, the abused, the maltreated, the exploited; no man had the right, not even a pharaoh, to enslave another, to murder the children of his opponents in order to establish himself and his own.

In the second passage, Exodus 6, a very remarkable incisive oracle, it is stated that Israel would know that Jahweh was its God by the deliverance from bondage, by the divine fellowship, and by the discoveries in the coming days.

> I am Jahweh
>
> I will bring you out from under the burdens of the Egyptians;
> I will deliver you from their bondage;
> I will redeem you with outstretched arm and with great acts of judgment.
>
> I will take you for my people;
> I will be your God;
> and you shall know that I am your God
> who has brought you out from under the burdens of the Egyptians.
>
> I will bring you into the land
> which I swore to give to Abraham, to Isaac, and to Jacob;
> I will give it to you for a possession.
>
> I am Jahweh.

If the contest with Pharaoh revealed the power and mercy of Jahweh, it unmasked the complete bankruptcy of Egyptian religion. Not only were the Egyptian gods utterly impotent to defend their devotees (cp. Judg. 9:46–49; 17:23–30; 1 Sam. 5:1–4), but one of their number, the regnant king of Egypt, was exposed in his irresponsible practices. It is instructive to see with what duplicity he acted during the plagues, how unreliable was his word, and how determined he was to perpetuate the oppression of Israel though all else be lost.

The first request of Moses, that Israel be permitted to sacrifice to Jahweh in the wilderness some three days' journey removed, Pharaoh countered with additional corvée assignments. While the Nile became as blood in the first plague, the magicians salved his conscience by producing a similar feat. When the frogs invaded the land, Pharaoh said: "Plead with Jahweh to remove the frogs from me and my people, and I will let the people go to sacrifice to Jahweh" (8:4). But when the frogs were no longer a threat, Pharaoh went back on his word.

When the fourth plague, that of the flies, occurred, Pharaoh summoned Moses and said, "Go and sacrifice to your God *within the land*" (8:21). Moses reasoned with the king that this were manifestly impossible because Israel's sacrifices would violate Egyptian religious sensibilities, and riots would no doubt result. Nevertheless, the king persisted in his demand, "I will let you go to sacrifice to Jahweh your God in the wilderness, but only *you shall not go very far.* Plead, then, for me" (8:28). The plague was removed, but the king reneged on his promise.

Enduring the murrain and the boils in stolid indifference, Pharaoh broke his silence when the hail fell. Summoning Moses and Aaron he confessed: "I stand guilty this time. Jahweh is in the right and I and my people are in the wrong. Plead with Jahweh; there has been enough of God's thunder and hail. I will let you go; you need stay no longer" (9:27 f.). When the storm ceased he reverted to type and withdrew permission.

When Moses threatened Egypt with an invasion of locusts, the courtiers issued a stern warning of the impending doom to his majesty. Calling Moses to court, Pharaoh proposed yet another inacceptable offer, "Go, worship Jahweh your God! Who are the ones to go?" (10:8). Moses explained that it was necessary that the entire community of Israel participate, young and old, sons and daughters, flocks and herds as well. The king responded with marked irritability. "And they were expelled from Pharaoh's presence." But when the locusts came, the king hurriedly called for Moses and acknowledged his guilt: "I stand guilty before Jahweh your God and before you. Forgive, then, my offense just this once, and plead with Jahweh your God that he but remove this death from me" (10:17). Again the pattern persisted: Pharaoh refused to let Israel go.

In the ninth plague, that of the sandstorm, Pharaoh remained obdurate. He suggested to Moses: "Go, worship Jahweh. Only your flocks and your herds shall be left behind; even your child may go with you!" (10:24). Moses reasoned that without the herds and flocks there could be no celebration of the feast; the herds and flocks must accompany the people, with no hoof left behind. Denying this request, Pharaoh retorted: "Be gone from me. Take care not to see me again, for the moment you look upon my face you shall die" (10:27).

Here was the glory of Egypt: the great god Pharaoh in all his splendor, unmasked in deceit, obduracy, and ethical irresponsibility. It is an exposure of the vaunted pretensions of Egypt, of an Egyptian king-god, of the impotence of Egyptian religion, and of the bankruptcy of Egyptian morality. The ultimate refutation of the crown was when Moses forecast that "all these courtiers of yours shall come down to me and bow low to me saying, 'Depart, you and your people who follow you!'" (11:8). The outcasts had arrived in their righteousness; and the proud diadem was fractured. Compared with the Egypt and its ways, how sublimely glorious was Jahweh in the moment of truth.

Theological Reflections. The contest with Pharaoh (4:27 to 6:1; 7:8 to 10:20) is the first major analysis in the Bible of the struggle of the people of God against humanistic world society. When contrasted with the community of God, world society is essentially humanistic. Its gods are nonexistent; its goals and practices, its motivation and character are determined and distorted by its lack of an ultimate ground of being. Its personnel, purposes, and plans necessarily derive from individual and societal egoism and share the limitation of their source. In the language of Exodus, the Pharaoh, ascribing to himself an inane status of a god, confronted the veritable God with the defiant question, "Who is Jahweh, that I should heed his voice? I do not know Jahweh" (5:2). The quotation serves very well as a point of departure in the ensuing conflict, for Pharaoh exhibited at every juncture his overbearing conceit and his abysmal ignorance of God.

That tension would arise between the people of God and world society is symbolically forecast in Genesis 3, where Jahweh indicates that there will be a continuing enmity between the woman and the serpent. In the ensuing mortal struggle the woman will be bruised in the heel, but the serpent in the head. Disrobed of its symbolism, the story predicts two societies locked in frightful combat. The people of God (the woman and her seed) must engage the rigors of the titanic struggle, must not yield to the blandishments of temptation as did the woman, and may be assured that the day will dawn when the enemy (the serpent and its heirs) will be defeated.

The contest with Pharaoh portrays the nature of the strife which will obtain when the kingdom of God and the kingdom of this world lock in opposition. It will be total war and total involvement of its participants in the head-on collision. The enemy will pursue his objectives oblivious of the common good and fiercely determined to win at all costs. His motivation may be irrational, the product of prejudice, hatred, vaunted privilege, passion, and lust; nowhere is morality to be sought. To succeed, the foe is willing to lose face, to compromise, to lie, to seduce, and to close his eyes in the face of incontestable truth. At his disposal are superior forces and the advantage is freighted in his favor, but when Jahweh enters the lists it spells an appropriate and humiliating defeat (compare 1 Sam. 6:6), a victory won by Jahweh alone but shared with his people.

The book of Revelation belongs to the apocalyptic writings and portrays the Christian faith in the resolution of history. Commencing with chapter 4 the book portrays in impressionistic symbolism the tension in history between the church and the world. Again and again it reiterates the gargantuan struggle with scenes set now in the camp of the enemy, now in the camp of the saints, with campaigns and attacks of the enemy and resistance by the church. In depicting the divine assault against the enemy, the author of the book of Revelation utilizes the motif of the Exodus plagues. Water turned to blood, boils, hail, locusts, and darkness are plagues in the divine arsenal of God. Five plagues are lifted from Exodus and infused in the text of Revelation.[13] But it is not that the plague motif of Exodus was alone borrowed; the framework of the struggle with Pharaoh was appropriated because it was a most suitable vehicle to exhibit the two worlds in conflict.

The New Testament conceives of two opposing ages: this present world and the world to come, and two opposing societies: the church and the world. Jesus assessed the enemy as "a strong man, fully armed, guarding his own palace with his goods in peace" (Luke 11:21). To those who aspired to become his disciples, Jesus warned that the contest would demand that total surrender that would mark a king engaging an army twice the size of his (Luke 14:31). The Christian experience is frequently described in terms of warfare. The church is to put on the whole armor of God for it wrestles against principalities and power, against the world rulers of this present darkness (Eph. 6:11–13). But the Christian soldier must not ape the weaponry of the enemy; rather he must use those spiritual weapons provided for him and so engage the foe with telling force (2 Cor. 10:3 f.). Despite the seeming weakness of his cause he may be assured that the ultimate victory will be Christ's (2 Cor. 2:14).

In the contest the bankruptcy of the enemy is unmasked, his despicable way, his foundationless boasts, his ruthless conduct, and his reprehensible duplicity. Pharaoh became for all time an egregious example of egocentric man, proud in mien, irresponsible in practice, tragic in fall. Jahweh, by contrast, demonstrates his transcendent power over nature and history, his long-suffering grace and goodness, his altruism and forbearance.

> I will send all my plagues upon your heart, and upon your servants and your people, that you may know that there is none like me in all the earth. For now I could have put forth my hand and struck you and your people with pestilence and you would have been cut off from the earth, but for this purpose have I let you live, to show you my power, so that my name may be declared throughout all the earth.
>
> (Ex. 9:15–16=Rom. 9:17)

It may be added that in the contest the gentle forbearance of Moses with the arrogant king was highlighted and became the ethical exemplar for the church in its dealings with its opponents.

NOTES

[1] The term *Egypt* is used in Hosea 8:13 and 9:3 symbolically to denote an incapacitating oppression.

[2] Compare this with the words of Paul concerning his visions: "whether in the body or out of the body I do not know" (2 Cor. 12:3,NEB).

[3] The removal of the sandals suggests that man has no essential standing room, no invested privilege, to stand in the divine presence (cp. Ruth 4:7 f.).

[4] The Israelites held that no one could see God ontically, that is, in his pure essence—that were beyond man's reach. But one could see God mediated in nature, history, or vision (cp. Ex. 24:10; Judg. 13:21 ff.; Isa. 6:1,5; 40:5). This phenomenal vision is the divine glory (Ps. 19:1).

[4a] Compare the "confessions of Jeremiah": 15:10–21; 17:1–4–18; 18:18–23; 20:7–13; 20:14–18; and in the New Testament: Luke 11:33; Hebrew 12:3.

[5] One must not imagine that the credence of the people here is contradicted by Exodus 6:9, where the people refuse to listen to Moses because of their woes. Exodus 6:2–7:7 is a supplement to Exodus 3:1 to 4:27. It embodies various fragments of the tradition, summary statements such as 6:13,26–27; 7:6–7 which have other settings than the continuous narrative of 3:1 to 4:27.

[6] A portion of the proceedings is recorded in Exodus 7:8–13, which should be read after Exodus 5:3.

[7] Notice the pretension to divinity existing at Tyre (Ezek. 28) and at Babylon (Isa. 14).

[8] Pritchard, ANET 416; cp. the Admonitions of Ipu-wer (ca. 2300–2050 B.C.) 5, iii.1. Ibid. 441. This attitude is quite normative in Egyptian history.

[9] *The Gathering Storm.* Boston: Houghton Mifflin Co., 1948,394.

[10] Compare this with an Egyptian text: "the River is blood. If one drinks of it, one rejects [it] . . . and thirsts for water" (ANET 441b).

[11] For similar irony see Judges 17:23 ff.; 1 Samuel 5:1 ff.; 6:6.

[12] Compare this with the admissions of Pharaoh in Exodus 9:27 f.; 10:16 f.

[13] Compare the first plague, water turned to blood, Exodus 7:20 with Revelation 16:3,4; the second plague, frogs, Exodus 7:25–8:15 with Revelation 16:4 (omitted above); the sixth plague, boils, Exodus 9:9 with Revelation 16:2,11; the seventh plague, hail, Exodus 9:23 with Revelation 8:7; 16:21; the eighth plague, locusts, Exodus 10:1 f. with Revelation 9:3,7; and the ninth plague, darkness, Exodus 10:21 with Revelation 16:10.

III

The Emancipation of Israel

(11—18)

These eight chapters present the story of the Passover, the Exodus, the journey to Mount Sinai, and other supportive materials.

A. The Passover (11:1 to 12:30)

1. Its Name. The term *passover* refers to an event, a festival, and a sacrifice. It is the translation of the Hebrew term *pesach*, a substantive derived from the verb *pasach* meaning to pass over. When the Old Testament was translated into Greek, it appeared as *pascha* (Latin *pascha*) and was introduced ca. A.D. 1200 to the English language in this transliterated form. It was not until 1530, in the translation of the Pentateuch by William Tyndale, that the translated form *passover* occurred.

2. Its Prelude (ch. 11). This chapter may be viewed as a dramatic arrest before the momentous events of the Passover are related. The intentional pause in the narrative, the rather extensive recall of Moses' last interview with Pharaoh, and the concluding summary are designed to build up the dramatic intensity to that which immediately follows.

There are three matters in the chapter which may be taken up here. The first is to point out that in verse 4 Moses delivered an oracle to Pharaoh even though the use of the third person obscures this to a degree. The second has to do with the ethical propriety of the Hebrews "despoiling the Egyptians" (3:21 f.; 11:2; 12:35 f.). The purpose of borrowing the jewelry and the clothing on the part of the Israelites was to present themselves in an appropriate garb before Jahweh when they celebrated the feast in the wilderness (cp. Ex. 33:4–6; Ex. 16:11). The legitimacy of the borrowing must be weighed against two considerations. The first is that notwithstanding the occasional goodwill of the Egyptians, the Israelites considered them essentially as enemies (15:6–7,9). The contest with Pharaoh is portrayed in polemic terms (Ex. 15); the Israelites joined the fray as the people of Jahweh equipped for battle (13:18) and marching defiantly (14:18) as an army (12:17,44,51). The jewelry and clothing were accounted as spoils of the battle, wherein Jahweh gloriously triumphed over his enemies (15:9; Ps. 105:37*a*; Josh. 22:8). They were scarce recompense for the years of oppression and servitude.

If one press the question further and take issue at the point of misrepresentation, the charge must be admitted. A Christian approach to this and similar problems is suggested by such a canon as Matthew 5:17–19 where the eternally valid and the temporal are separated and where the test of the former is Christological. The rhetorical art of the Old Testament couched priestly and prophetic utterances as divine (cp. 1 Sam. 14:36 ff.; 25:3; 21:1 ff.). A similar situation appears indicated in the oracles regarding "spoiling the Egyptians." An unethical complicity has no revelational quality where Christ is Lord of the Scriptures and the materials under review must be adjudged in this light.

The second matter has to do with the meaning of the word *firstborn.* The problem may be seen in Exodus 4:22–23: "You shall say to Pharaoh, 'Thus says Jahweh, Israel is my first-born son, and I say to you, Let my son go that he may serve me; if you refuse to let him go, behold, I will slay your first-born son' " (RSV). In the first place, all notions of biological sonship must be excluded in the relationship between Jahweh and Israel. *Son* is a caritative term, one of endearment, betokening that those close ties existent between a father and a son are vis-a-vis similar to that attachment existent between Jahweh and Israel. Secondly, the term *firstborn* in its physical sense occurs in Exodus 12 and 13 quite frequently and colors the pattern of thought. Thirdly, there are figurative extensions of the father-son relationship, whether it be the king as the adopted son of Jahweh (2 Sam. 7:14; Ps. 2:7), or, as here, the people of Israel. In this particular passage one could argue that the word *firstborn* signifies "people" in verse 22 and should have the same meaning in verse 23 so that, laying aside the metaphor, it might be translated as "behold, I will slay your people."

Fourthly, it is not characteristic of epidemics, and the Passover was essentially a plague, to restrict themselves to the firstborn of men and cattle. Of course, one could argue that it was a divine visitation and cannot be judged by the normal course an epidemic. But in every plague, including the plague of the firstborn, the natural data are described to such a degree that they cannot be dismissed forthwith (compare Ex. 23:25; Deut. 28:27,35,60). Fifthly, if we consider the word *firstborn* as equivalent to people, some support for this opinion may be found in Psalm 78:51, where in parallel relationship to *firstborn* is "the first issue of their strength;" and in Wisdom of Solomon 18:15, where the counterpart is "their most valued children." It is, therefore, suggested that the plague of the firstborn was an epidemic affecting the young and associated with the murrain. In the epidemic of sweating sickness that swept over England in 1528 there were striking similarities between the murrain among cattle and the sweating sickness among men. Be that as it may, Exodus 11 provides a break in the action and serves by its respite to create a mounting anticipation for the next dramatic movement.

3. The Event (12:1–30). The Passover is immediately singled out as something quite extraordinary in that it would mark the beginning of a new calendar. The Egyptian New Year was July 20, the beginning of the inundation. The event to be narrated in Exodus 12 is so significant that it will inaugurate a new beginning for Israel.

The ritual attending this event prescribed that each family select on the tenth day of Abib (March-April) a year old lamb or goat without blemish. On the fourteenth day of the same month, at twilight, the animal was to be slain, its blood caught in a basin and applied with hyssop to the two doorposts and lintel of each house. The flesh was then to be roasted in fire, spiced with bitter herbs, and eaten with unleavened bread. Whatever remained was to be burned. Family units too small to consume an entire lamb or goat shared the ritualistic meal with their neighbors. The participants of

Jahweh's Passover were to be girded, with sandals on their feet, and staff in hand, eating it with dispatch and awe (12:1–11). The paschal lamb remained intact during the cooking (12:9); no bones were to be broken, and no portion of the flesh was to be removed from the premises. It has been suggested that these ritualistic details symbolized the protection of the wholeness of those participating, the soundness and togetherness of the group for whom the lamb was sacrificed.

With the people fed and prepared to march, the long awaited and final confrontation of Jahweh with Egypt and her gods took place. It is described in two levels: there was the divine aspect of the event portraying Jahweh as immediately involved in invading the land of Egypt, smiting the firstborn of the Egyptians, both man and cattle, but passing over the houses of the Israelites which were sprinkled with blood (12:12–13,23,27,29). The other aspect describes the phenomenal level: it is identified as a plague of severe intensity occasioned by the destroyer entering and smiting the houses unmarked by blood (12:13,23). The Old Testament includes both the divine and the phenomenal in its descriptions of plagues (2 Sam. 5:6,9,12; 6:4 f.; 24:15–17,21,25) and famines (1 Sam. 21:1,10). It is an affirmation on their part that God is behind every event (Amos 3:6*b*), a recognition that he uses proximate means to effect his will (Isa. 10:5 ff.; 2 Sam. 23:12). The two phases of the Passover event are represented in Psalm 78:49–51:

> He let loose on them his fierce anger,
> wrath, indignation, and distress,
> a company of destroying angels.
> He made a path for his anger;
> he did not spare them from death,
> but gave their lives over to the *plague*.
> He smote all the first-born in Egypt,
> the first issue of their strength in
> the tents of Ham.

When the last plague invaded Egypt with its unspeakable horror, the Egyptians, tormented by the repeated disasters of the previous months, became frantic as the epidemic raged. "Egypt was glad when they departed, for dread of them had fallen upon it" (Ps. 105:38). Forthwith the court issued the decree for Israel to depart from Egypt immediately with their possessions. So urgent was the royal command, the Israelites had to take their sour dough before it was risen; and, with the jewelry and clothing as a parting gift (Mic. 1:14) from the Egyptians, they evacuated at once the land of their sojourn (12:31–36).

4. The Antecedents of the Passover. Moses and Aaron assumed the religious leadership of Israel from the time Moses reentered Egypt to deliver Israel. They inherited the patriarchal religious practices and built upon them. This is illustrated by the fact that Moses initially requested the release of Israel to celebrate a feast to Jahweh in the wilderness with appropriate sacrifices "lest he fall upon us with pestilence or with the sword" (Ex. 5:3). Moreover, it would appear that Moses had a tent of meeting marked by the divine presence (33:7–10) and the sacred fire, and where oracles were obtained (18:7,15) and in which a pot of manna was placed before Jahweh, that is, before the testimony, which may be conceived to be the prototype of the ark of the covenant (16:33).

The Passover was essentially an ancient ritual of nomadic shepherds whereby the welfare of the flock might be secured through ritual sacrifice ere the shepherds commenced their spring migrations. Omission of this apotropaic service would expose the community to "the destroyer" (5:3; 12:23) whether plague or sword (cp. Ps. 91:3,6). The Israelites shared with the nomadic shepherds the same calling in life (Gen. 46:32–4; 47:3), sacrificed the same animals (note the contrasting difference of the Egyptian practice in Ex. 8:26), roasted food over a fire without kitchen utensils, seasoned meals with wild herbs gathered from the wilderness, ate often on the march or hurriedly, and drove their flocks annually to spring pasture. It is not surprising that a protective ritual—not altogether dissimilar to the blessing of the fishing fleets in the Low Countries by the Catholic clergy—should initiate their emigration for spring pasture lands.

This annual, spring ritual of the nomadic or seminomadic shepherds was no doubt part and parcel of the religious legacy of

Israel. Building upon that which was familiar, the inspired leader of Israel adapted the earlier ritual to the new set of circumstances now confronting the oppressed Israelites.

The Passover ritual served admirably as the initiatory ritual for the momentous occasion. It comprehended within itself the judgment of the impenitent oppressor, the protection and release for an Israel now bound for the promised land, and a sacrament readily understood by its participants and worthy of perpetual observance (Ex. 12:24–27; Ps. 81:1–5). Its celebration was subsequently enlarged to include purchased slaves and resident aliens provided they were circumcised. (Ex. 12:43–49).

5. The Feast of Unleavened Bread/Massoth (Ex. 12:14–20): When the book of Exodus was ultimately brought together, it combined various types of literature from various sources and times into its present form. In the same chapter will be found narrative, ritual, and legal materials. In Exodus 12 the greater part of the chapter is given over to the *narrative* of the Passover, but in verses 24–27 there is a *prescription* for its continued observance while in 14–15, 16–20, and 13:3–10 the ritual for the observance of the feast of unleavened bread is thrice presented.

The sequence of development would appear to have developed in some such form as the following: (1) The extreme haste urged upon the Israelites by the frenzied Egyptians provided no occasion for the daily sour dough to rise in the kneading bowls when Israel left Egypt. Accordingly, the emigrants baked unleavened cakes for their sustenance. (2) This feature of the total Exodus experience was then to be partially reenacted as a memorial of the solemn occasion. (3) The passover was celebrated on the fourteenth of Abib; the feast of unleavened bread was to be observed from the fifteenth to the twenty-second, with the first and seventh to be observed as sabbaths. *Massoth* ("feast of unleavened bread") was not an agricultural feast, as is often erroneously asserted; it was instituted solely as a festal week commemorating the exodus from Egypt. It permitted the descendants of those who originally shared in the exodus to identify with the experience sacramentally by eating unleavened bread, nostalgically named, the bread of affliction (Ex. 12:3–10).

Theological Reflections. The Passover may be viewed from two points. For the Egyptians it spelled doom and disaster, a judgment slowly but surely incurred by their heartless and ruthless treatment of the Israelites. Judgment is never pleasant; it conjures up the deep regret that it has to be, but it must needs to be administered if life is to have meaningfulness and continuance. Paul formulated in Romans 2:3–6,11 a classic expression which well illustrates the necessity for the judgment of Egypt.

> Do you suppose, O man, . . . you will escape the judgment of God? Or do you presume upon the riches of his kindness and forbearance and patience? Do you not know that God's kindness is meant to lead you to repentance? But by your hard and impenitent heart you are storing up wrath for yourself on the day of wrath when God's righteous judgment will be revealed. For he will render to every man according to his works. . . . God shows no partiality (RSV).

In the relevant discussion the divine patience and long suffering have been pointed out. Nevertheless, the plagues were not without redemptive worth, as is noted in the words of Jahweh to Pharaoh: "For this purpose have I let you live, to show you my power, so that my name may be declared throughout all the earth" (Ex. 9:16). Unfortunately, the invisible nature of Jahweh, namely, his eternal power and deity, though clearly perceivable in the signs and wonders performed, was denied by the impenitent Egyptian heart. Naught else was left but judgment.

From the Israelite point of view the judgment of God broke the logjam of injustice and oppression and released righteousness and redemption for the maltreated and abused. The Passover was a red-letter day in the history of Israel and was thereafter a cardinal feast in their religious calendar (Ex. 12:1–13,43–49; Lev. 23:4–8; Num. 9:1–14; 28:16–25).

The Passover and the Feast of Unleavened Bread are of major importance in the New Testament. The last supper Jesus ate with his disciples was the celebration of the Passover meal. Expressions derived from the passover observance are woven into the thought of the Christian tradition. Jesus is "the Lamb of God" (John 1:29,36) and is portrayed some twenty-seven times in the book of Revelation under the symbol of a lamb. Peter reminds his readers that they were redeemed with the precious blood of Christ, as of a lamb without blemish or spot (1 Pet. 1:19; cp. Ex. 12:5). And John records that the usual breaking of the bones of one crucified under Roman jurisdiction was waived so that Jesus exemplified more perfectly the paschal lamb (John 19:36; cp. Ex. 12:46).

Paul adapted the Passover and the Feast of Unleavened Bread to a Christian perspective in 1 Corinthians 5:6–8.

> Your boasting is not good. Do you not know that a little leaven ferments the whole lump of dough? Cleanse out the old leaven that you may be fresh dough, as you really are unleavened. For Christ, our [passover] paschal lamb, has been sacrificed. Let us, therefore, celebrate the festival, not with the old leaven, the leaven of malice and evil, but with the unleavened bread of sincerity and truth (RSV).

In these words Paul affirms that Christianity is a feast, that Jesus Christ is the veritable passover (=paschal lamb), which has been sacrificed for us, and that we have become a new lump (Christian unity) and truly leavened (Christian salvation). The term *leaven* is used in this passage in a negative sense; it is used symbolically to mean malice and evil, whereas unleavened bread signifies sincerity and truth. It is an exhortation to observe the ancient Feast of Unleavened Bread in its Christian reinterpretation. Leave in Egypt the leaven of the old life, malice and evil, and have no more to do with its proliferating power. Remember it was Christ our paschal lamb that redeemed you therefrom, and now let us keep the feast with lives of sincerity and truth for that is the purpose of the observance.

B. The Exodus (12:32 to 15:21)

The exodus itself commenced from Raamses in the land of Goshen (Ex. 12:37; Gen. 47:11) with the first encampment at Succoth, somewhere in the general vicinity of the eastern part of Wadi Tumilat. Excitement must have reigned in the camp of Israel as guides and drivers, wagons and pack animals converged to swell the numbers. With flocks and herds in droves, with all types of traveling conveyance, and with the crowds of men, women, children, and foreigners, all anxiously awaited the signal to move. The number of participants is given as 600,000 males, but the logistics of the situation suggest that the total number could not have been some two million. Most investigators have proposed between 6,000 and 60,000 for the total number involved. Perhaps within these two limits a reliable estimate can be made.[1]

Between Exodus 12:36 and 13:16, where the new narrative section commences, there are four sections of materials each specifically defined in the Hebrew text (Ex. 12:37–42; 43–51; 13:1–16) and having the nature of addenda. These four sections are rather self-contained units of supplementary character whether historical or ritual. It may provide an insight into the liturgical practices of Judaism in that where a major pericope ends, additional materials, not integral but related to the foregoing, were included.

The ritual for the Feast of Unleavened Bread and for the redemption of the firstborn have identical phrasing in two instances. Both presuppose the day when a son will ask his father the reason for the ceremony; both provide the same answer: "It is because of what Jahweh did for me when I went free from Egypt" (Ex. 13:8,14). Moreover, both ceremonies are to be observed as a sign would be on one's hand and as a reminder on one's forehead (13:9,16; cp. Deut. 6:20 ff.). These passages together with such as Genesis 18:19; Exodus 10:2; 12:26 f. are important for the catechetical development in Israel, or to put it another way, the religious education program.

Mention has already been made of the Feast of Unleavened Bread; what remains to be discussed is the redemption of the firstborn (Ex. 13:11–16). In primitive Semitic religion it is a reasonable inference that the firstborn male belonged to the deity. Child sacrifice and indirect references to the sacrifice of the firstborn (Gen. 22; 1 Kings 3:27; Mic. 6:7) support this idea. It must be borne in mind that Israel fell heir to a Sumero-Akkadian culture and that Abram's forebears were polytheistic pagans (Josh. 24:14 f.,20,23). Jahwism purified the ritual in showing that all progeny belonged to God but were not to be sacrificed. In Exodus 13:11–16 the firstborn of men are to be redeemed by a votive offering, the firstborn of animals by the prescribed sacrifice (v. 12 f.). It is an instance of the effective purification Jahwism enjoined upon its worshipers of a pagan practice that in every respect was horrendous.

1. The Passage Through the Sea (Ex. 13:17 to 14:31) A recurring theme of the march of Israel is the pillar of cloud by day and of fire by night occurring in the book of Exodus eight times (13:21 twice, 22 twice; 14:19, 24; 33:9 f.). The pillar may fairly be conceived as the enveloping insignia of Jahweh, the standard that provided direction for the march and halt of Israel by its light moving in the darkness and its visible column (of smoke) during the day. The renowned Arabist, C. H. Doughty, describes a caravan pilgrimage of some 6,000 participants and 10,000 animals of all types from Damascus to Mecca in his famous work, *Travels in Arabia Deserta.* The pilgrim caravan of 1876, of which he was a member, proceeded with the principals in the van, followed by the slow-footed multitude of men and cattle stretching out some two miles in length and covering some one hundred yards in width in the open plains. Forced marches at night set out at three-thirty o'clock. "The night sky was dark and showery when we removed, and cressets of iron cages set upon poles were borne to light the way, upon serving men's shoulders." This time-honored means to guide a host at night was used by Alexander the Great. As he went through Babylonia, "he set a pole which could be seen on every side, over the royal tent, which showed a signal conspicuous to all, seen as fire by night and as smoke by day." So reports Quintus Curtius, a Roman historian of the first century A.D. Dean Henry Alford affirms that Jahweh "may have been pleased to base upon an existing practice His method of manifesting His guarding and leading presence to His people." This view is strengthened when it is remembered that the sacrificial fire was not to go out (Lev. 6:12 f.); it is called the "perpetual fire" (1 Esdras 6:24). The continuity of the sacred fire must needs be maintained; other means of igniting the fire for sacrifice was "strange fire" (Lev. 10:1,2). It is suggested that this fire was carried in a brazier in the van of the march and was revered as the symbolic presence of Jahweh. It is called a "pillar," which in Hebrew means "a column" and is normally equivalent to a column of smoke (Judg. 20:40). "In the daytime he led them with a cloud, and all the night with a fiery light [lit., 'light of fire']"(Ps. 78:14).

When Israel left Egypt, it avoided as far as possible contact with the "way of the land of the Philistines," for that was the famous Egyptian military road leading from the east delta to Raphia in the land of Canaan and buttressed with fortresses. Israel had encamped first at Succoth, then at Etham, and finally, before the passage through the sea, at Pi-hahiroth (Egyptian: *Pr-Hthr*, "the house of [the goddess] Hathor") at which location it had arrived by retreating along the wilderness at the Sea of Reeds.[2] Such a turning back may suggest that Israel was about to encounter Egyptian troops stationed along the eastern border country who would consider the flight as an unwarranted escape. Fronting the sea on the east, flanked by the wilderness and perchance the Egyptian frontier guard, Israel was vulnerable to a rear attack. The narrative strongly intimates that this was the situation in which helpless Israel was to witness the divine salvation and wherein the Egyptians would experience the power of Jahweh (14:2,4).

In the terror of the epidemic of the firstborn, the panic-stricken Egyptians released Israel from the oppressive subjugation it had imposed upon a resident-alien minority; but permitting Israel to emigrate had serious labor and economic consequences for the Egyptians. To lose such a valuable labor force imperiled the agricultural facilities of the land and abruptly curtailed building supplies for government projects. The calculating crown repented of the hasty decision, ordered into action its elite chariotry, and advanced toward the fugitives at Pi-hahiroth fronting the sea.

When the Israelite scouts reported the oncoming attack of the crack Egyptian chariotry, the people were dismayed and struck out blindly at Moses with three disdainful questions. The first is a parade example of the sardonic: "Was it for want of graves in Egypt that you have brought us to die in the wilderness?" The second decries the fatuous nature of his mission: "What have you done to us taking us out of Egypt?" The final attack repudiates the entire program of liberation: "Is this not the very thing we told you in Egypt, saying, 'Let us be, and we will serve the Egyptians, for it is better for us to serve the Egyptians than to die in the wilderness'?" The very punch line of the people opposing Moses in Egypt is here preserved in the quotation. The motley fugitives were in frantic disarray.

Over against this sorry picture rises the grandeur of Moses: first, interceding for divine direction, then ordering the people to march to the shores of the sea, there to discover the power of God over the Egyptian foe and to avail themselves of an exodus through the sea. As the people marched toward the sea, the leader with the divine insignia moved from the van to protect the rear. And now it happened! Before their very eyes unfolded one of the significant moments in human history, an event equally singular for the magnificent anticipation of Moses: "Fear not! Stand still, and witness the deliverance which Jahweh will work for you today; for the Egyptians whom you see today, you will never see again. Jahweh will fight for you; hold then your peace!" (14:13 f.).

During that night a strong east wind arose driving back the waters from the sands of the shallow shoals, and through the Sea of Reeds, flanked by waters on both sides, the Israelites fled safely to the opposite shore (14:21 f.). The Egyptians attempted the same passage some hours later, but the wind shifted southward following the morning watch [3] (two to six A.M.), enmeshing the chariot wheels and engulfing the pursuing host in the returning waters (14:24 ff.; 15:10). The sober morning dawned; the foe had been completely routed; Jahweh had triumphed over the proudest in the cause of liberty. His servant Moses had been vindicated and was now recognized as the proven leader of Israel. Everything had suddenly become new: the year, the leader, the political status; as freemen Israel moved into a new dimension of that hope vouchsafed by Jahweh to their fathers.

In its narrowest dimension the Isthmus of Suez, within whose borders occurred the crossing through the sea, extends northward from the Gulf of Suez in the Red Sea some seventy miles to the Mediterranean. This unique land bridge from Africa to Asia is now intersected by the Suez Canal which proceeds from Suez in the south to Port Said on the Mediterranean in the north, a nautical distance of some 101 miles. When M. de Lesseps began to build the Suez Canal in 1859, though its antecedents can be traced back to canal-building pharaohs as early as 2000 B.C., its topographical components were as follows: (1) a lagoon, several miles in length, extending north of the Gulf of Suez; (2) the *Shaluf*, a plateau some six miles long; (3) the two Bitter Lakes, later to extend some twenty-five miles in a northwest direction; (4) the Serapeum, an intersecting stretch of sand, some eight miles long; (5) Lake Timsah, five miles in length; (6) *El Gisr* ("the Embankment"), where the land rises about fifty feet above the sea and extends some six miles; (7) Lakes Ballah; (8) El Qantarah, a narrow land crossing, the starting point of "the way of the Philistines," one of the oldest highways in the world; [4] and (9) Lake Menzaleh extending some twenty-seven and a half miles to Port Said.

If one looks at this terrain, the question arises as to why Moses confronted his people with a water mass, when there were three land bridges available (Nos. 2, 4, 6 above), particularly when he must have known the Egyptian topography. This problem is soon put to rest by considering that the physical features of the territory have been significantly changed during the past three millennia. The Bitter Lakes and Lake Timsah were scarcely more than large salt marshes before 1862. In the construction of the Suez Canal the Mediterranean flowed into Lake Timsah in 1862 while the Red Sea poured its waters into the Bitter Lakes, enormously increasing their size in 1869. The *Shaluf* (No. 2 above) and *El Gisr* (No. 6) are largely products of the shifting sands of the surrounding arid region. Moreover, there is strong geological and archaeological evidence that the Gulf of Suez extended inland as far as Lake Timsah in the period under review.

Scholars have proposed several localities for the Israelitic crossing; (1) Near modern Suez, either in the narrow north arm of the Gulf, some three-fourths of a mile wide; or south of Suez where a shoal occurs, quite shallow at ebb tide; (2) Along the northern extension of the ancient Gulf of Suez: a little north of Serapeum (No. 4 above) or south of the Little Bitter Lake (No. 3). Our inability to reconstruct the actual course of events and to identify the exact locale results from the absence of available data and from topographical changes in the region, but "the *fact* of the passage of the Red Sea can be questioned only by an extreme and baseless skepticism" (S. R. Driver).

The passage of Israel through the Sea of Reeds, for this is its proper name in the twenty-eight instances occurring in the Old Testament, is recounted in prose (ch. 14) and in poetry (ch. 15). The Passover-Exodus event is the cornerstone in the religion of Israel. It was a revelation of Jahweh in history, in nature, and in ethics. The impression it made on the consciousness of Israel became definitive; it was a cardinal affirmation in the catechism of Israel rehearsed over and again in the historical books (Judg. 6:8,9,13; 1 Sam. 12:6,8; 1 Kings 8:51), celebrated in the liturgy of the psalms (78:13; 114:1,3; 106: 7–11), and adduced in its theological significance in the stirring words of the prophets (Hos. 11:1; Jer. 7:21 ff.; 11:1 ff; Isa. 10:24,26).

2. The Song at the Sea (Ex. 15). The stunning victory of Jahweh over the Egyptians and the resultant jubilation in Israel evoked a fitting response in song. Replete with the elements of the astounding event, the song is a victory paean or epinicean ode, much like the later Song of Deborah. Miriam, the sister of Moses and Aaron, initiated the actual rendition of the composition with timbrel and dance accompaniment (cp. 1 Sam. 18: 6–7). That she is called a prophetess (15:20) coincides with an early nuance of the Hebrew verb *n-b-'*, which, normally translated "prophesy," has here the meaning "to sing in exultant mood," and as such is found in 1 Samuel 10:6,10. The song was sung with challenge by one group to evoke a response from the other. The challenge is framed in the imperative; it seeks to elicit a worthy answer. Thus Miriam and the women of Israel with dance and timbrel sang:

> "*Sing* to Jahweh, for he has triumphed gloriously;
> horse and driver he has hurled into the sea" (15:21)

The men then repeated the words lustily. Thereupon the song depicts the phases of the great triumph.

The composition may be divided into two stanzas or responses: verses 1–10 and 11–18. Each begins with a doxological introduction

(vv. 1–3, 11) and continues by particularizing the motivating causes for the praise (vv. 4–10, 12–18). The first stanza depicts the triumphs of the past; the second projects from the past to the future.

The first response (15:1–10). In the introductory formulae of hymnic praise Jahweh is extolled for his glorious triumph in bold anthropomorphisms from the vocabulary of warfare. The singer identifies Jahweh the warrior (v. 3) with the God of the fathers (3:14 f.) and owns him as his God, his strength, his might, his salvation (vv. 1–3).

The poem then focuses attention on the shattering defeat inflicted upon the haughty Egyptians. The high and mighty, Pharaoh's chariots, the elite corps, sank ignominously into the depths of the sea: they drowned in the Sea of Reeds, the depths covered them; they went down into the depths like a stone! Its sardonic irony is intensified by repetition (cp. Judg. 5:27).

What occasioned such a disaster? The poet explains.

> Thy right hand, Jahweh, glorious in power,
> Thy right hand, Jahweh, shatters the enemy.
> In the greatness of thy majesty
> thou overthrowest thy adversaries;
> Thou sendest forth thy fury,
> it consumes them like stubble.
> At the blast of thy nostrils,
> the waters piled up,
> the floods stood in a heap;
> the deeps congealed in the heart of the sea (Ex. 15:6–8).

The poet then rehearses the audacious boast of the foe, and follows it with the climactic nemesis: "You made your wind blow; the sea covered them; They sank like lead in the majestic waters" (v. 10). We may imagine that these words were immediately greeted by the animated response of the women with their paean of praise challenging again the male chorus to proceed with the song.

The second response (15:11–18). As has been noted, this stanza commences with an hymnic introduction in which the incomparableness of Jahweh is stressed (cp. Ps. 30:4; 104:24; 108:5; 113:5). None among the gods (*sic!*) is like Jahweh. To compare Jahweh with these pagan nonentities is to demonstrate that there is *nothing* in common between them (Ps. 86:8; 89:5 ff.). Jahweh alone is majestic in holiness, that is, in that which is essentially Deity; awesome in glorious deeds, that is, when he enters the arena of history with his wonders.

The poet hurriedly summarizes the triumph in his eagerness to draw its implications for the future. Jahweh's love and strength led the redeemed people to freedom; and he did it in such a way that other nations posing a menace to Israel now will hear his wonders and be more amenable than were the Egyptians (Num. 14:13 ff.; Ex. 32:11 ff.; Num. 23:22; Josh. 2:10 f.; 5:1; 1 Sam. 4:7 f.). The inhabitants of Canaan, the Moabites, Edomites, and those in Philistia, are stunned by the news that has come out of Egypt. If Israel will but buy this vision, the future will be theirs, that is, the land of Canaan and the role Israel was elected to fulfill.

The purpose of the song was to glorify Jahweh in his redemptive mercy for the liberation of an oppressed people who were destined to bless mankind. To regard it as a gloat over the Egyptians, an imperious disdain of the nations in Canaan, is to mistake the accidental for the essential.

Theological Reflections. The passage through the sea is in one sense the exodus proper, the climax of Israel's redemption from Egypt, but in another sense it is but a part of the larger salvation. Preparation, plagues, Passover as well as provision, covenant, law, and worship are integral parts of Israel's exodus heritage. In the circumstances the term *exodus* has a greater content than the mere passage through the sea.

It is not necessary to dwell on the mighty power of Jahweh that made a way in the sea, a path in the mighty waters (Isa. 43:16) or to dilate the triumphant faith of Moses against the dark backdrop of the people's unbelief. What may not be readily apparent is the influence the exodus experience had in Israel's history.

The exodus assumed a high moment in the praises of Israel, not only in the Song of Miriam but in the book of Psalms.

Come and see what God has done:
he is terrible in his deeds among men.
He turned the sea into dry land;
men passed through the river on foot (Ps. 66:5 f.).

Thy way was through the sea,
thy path through the great waters;
yet thy footprints were unseen.
Thou didst lead thy people like a flock
by the hand of Moses and Aaron (Ps. 77:19 f.).[5]

The inexpressible joy of emancipation may be gathered from the Israelites who experienced the "second exodus."

When Jahweh restored the fortunes of Zion,
we were like those who dream.
Then our mouth was filled with laughter,
and our tongue with shouts of joy;
then they said among the nations,
"Jahweh has done great things for them."
Jahweh has done great things for us;
we are glad (Ps. 126:1–3).

The exodus theme plays an important role in the prophetic thought. It is referred to as one of the towering peaks of Israel's experience with Jahweh, the magnificent revelation of Jahweh, when he bared his arm in redemptive power and all flesh beheld it together. The event is singled out because of its importance and is joined to the oracular introduction: "Thus said Jahweh who brought thee up out of the land of Egypt," not merely because of the importance of the past event, but because it bridges the past with the present: "Jahweh who brought the sons of Israel out of the land of Egypt—the God who exhibited himself in that stupendous event—is the same God who now speaks *to you.*" It is in this thought pattern that Jeremiah writes: "Therefore, behold the days come, says Jahweh, when it shall no longer be said, 'As Jahweh lives who brought up the people of Israel out of the land of Egypt,' but 'As Jahweh lives who brought up the people of Israel out of the north country and out of all the countries where he had driven them' " (Jer. 16:14–15 = 23:7–8). This word of God was directed to the Babylonian exiles assuring them that Jahweh was a God of exoduses, that the God who broke the bars of the Egyptian enslavement would direct the same energies toward the Babylonian captivity. One and the same God ever multiplying the exodus experience for his people! The second exodus is more fully described in Isaiah 43:16,19–21:

> Thus says Jahweh,
> who opened a way in the sea
> and a path through mighty waters, . . .
> Here and now I will do a new thing;
> this moment it will break from the bud.
> Can you not perceive it?
> I will make a way even through the wilderness
> and paths in the barren desert . . . .
> I will provide water in the wilderness,
> and rivers in the barren desert . . . .
> where my chosen people may drink.
> I have formed this people for myself;
> they shall proclaim my praises.

The insistence here is that God is the same yesterday, today, and forever. He is the eternal Contemporary, the God not merely of the past, but of the present; not One who did great wonders in history, but the God who does wonders in the here and now.

In harmony with this thought the New Testament portrays Christian salvation in terms of redemption through the blood of the Lamb (Rev. 5:6,9; 1 Pet. 1:19). In the transfiguration Jesus spoke with Moses and Elijah concerning his "exodus" which he was to accomplish at Jerusalem (Luke 9:31). Paul describes very clearly what the Christian exodus is. He writes:

> I want you to know, brethren, that our fathers were all under the cloud, and all passed through the sea, and all were baptized into Moses in the cloud and in the sea, and all ate the same supernatural food and all drank the same supernatural drink. For they drank from the supernatural Rock which followed them, and the Rock was Christ. (1 Cor. 10: 1–5).

In the fulfillment of that ancient exodus, the Christian affirms his allegiance to Christ (the pillar of cloud), receives baptism in relationship to his new leader in the context of forgiveness and enduement, and attends the spiritual nurture provided by the everpresent Christ. The sea we traverse may be mingled with fire, yet we pass through it with the song of Moses and the Lamb ringing in our hearts (Rev. 15:3).

C. En Route To Sinai (Ex. 15:22 to 18:26)

This block of materials describes the major events which occurred in Israel's journey from the Sea of Reeds to Sinai. It may be conveniently divided into three sections: (1) From the Sea to Elim (15:22–27); (2) In the Wilderness of Sin (ch. 16); and (3) At Rephidim (chs. 17—18).

1. From the Sea to Elim (15:22–27). It is quite impossible for one living in the temperate zone to imagine the severities and hardships that confront one who attempts to survive in the semidesert aridity of Sinai. Francois-Michel de Roziere, a French engineer who accompanied Napoleon to Egypt in 1798, contrasted the erstwhile home of Israel in the delta with the barrenness of the Isthmus of Suez. He described the Nile Delta as "a cool plain, crossed in all directions by running water, shaded with palms and clothed in verdure, flowers and rich harvests." Then he wrote: "But journey on to the Isthmus, and under the same sky, all around is changed; no trace of cultivation, no houses, no shade, no greenery, no running streams, in short, nothing of use to man or beast; search the vast horizon as you may, there is nothing to arrest the eye from sea to sea, but parched and lifeless deserts, bare rocks, glaring sands and utterly arid plains." [6] In the book of Deuteronomy the terrain is described as "a great and terrible wilderness, with its fiery serpents and scorpions and thirsty ground, where there was no water." (Deut. 8:15; Jer. 2:6). Israel deprecated its inhospitality in stronger language: "Why have you made us come up out of Egypt, to bring us to this evil place? It is no place for grain, or figs, or vines, or pomegranates; and there is no water to drink" (Num. 20:5). Given these ingredients, one can easily see trouble ahead.

Marching southeast from the Sea of Reeds through the wilderness of Shur, with their water supplies exhausted, they arrived at Marah, where the water was so brackish that it was undrinkable. When the people complained, Moses was instructed to sweeten the waters by casting into them a tree.

This trial was the beginning of the divine tutelage, a lesson at once painful yet profitable (Deut. 8). Sluch experiences, intimated the leader, would become a fixed pattern to test the mettle of the people.

> It was there that Jahweh laid down a precept and rule of life, and bid them put it to the test. He said, "If only you will obey Jahweh your God, if you will do what is right in his eyes, if you will listen to his commands and keep all his statutes, then I will never bring upon you any of the sufferings which I was forced to bring on the Egyptians; for I am Jahweh who is your healer" (Ex. 15:25 f.).

After Marah they came to the oasis of Elim and luxuriated at the twelve springs beneath seventy palm trees!

2. ***In the Wilderness of Sin (ch. 16).*** On the fifteenth day of the second month of their journey the Israelites began to move eastward into the hill country of the Wilderness of Sin. Inexperienced in such rigorous demands and forced to a subsistence diet, the people again gave vent to their discontent: "If only we had died by the hand of Jahweh in the land of Egypt, when we sat by the fleshpots, when we ate our fill of bread! For you have brought us out into this wilderness to starve this whole congregation to death" (16:3). It was an utterance of deep despair, a nostalgic wish critical of Moses and his fatuous utopianism. Whether in Egypt or in the wilderness, they argued, we appear doomed to die; better then to die in Egypt with stomachs full than to die in the wilderness of starvation.

If Moses had no other virtue, he would be a prince among men for his patient understanding of his querulous people.

In an analysis of the chapter there is, first of all, a series of oracles vouchsafed to Moses, three given directly (vv. 4,5, 11–12, 28–29) and two obliquely (vv. 16, 32). In the first oracle Jahweh promised Moses that he would cause bread to rain down for Israel from heaven. The people were to go out and gather each day that day's portion, and on the sixth day it would prove to be twice as much as they gathered on other days; thus it would sustain them on the sabbath. Here, then, is a pre-Mosaic sabbath commandment.

The second oracle grows out of the confrontation of Jahweh and the congregation of Israel on the morning following the dissatisfaction of the people. Jahweh affirmed that flesh and bread would be provided, mighty acts betokening that it was he who brought them out of the land of Egypt and reassuring them that he was their God (vv. 11–12; cp. Hos. 12:9; 13:4).

The third oracle portrays anthropomorphically in a reproachful question the impatience of Jahweh with those of Israel who refused to follow his instructions concerning the gathering of the manna and reiterates the direction that two days' food would be provided the sixth day so that none would be engaged in work on the sabbath (vv. 28–29). Again the observance of the sabbath appears before the Ten Commandments were given.

The two obliquely communicated oracles have reference to the manna, the first having to do with the amount to be gathered (v. 16), while the other enjoins the preservation of one omer of manna as a testimony to posterity (v. 32). Aaron placed the memorial before the "Testimony" (v. 34). Here mention is made of a "Testimony," presumably some prototype of the ark of testimony (cp. Ex. 25:16; 30:36).

The second stratum of the narrative is the word of Moses to the congregation. First, he met the opposition of the grumblers with a three-pronged rejoinder: (1) tomorrow will be a confrontation with Jahweh; (2) he will give you flesh and bread; and (3) the conflict is not with him but between Jahweh and them (vv. 6–8). Secondly, Moses led the people to the Presence of Jahweh and mediated the oracle of promised flesh and food from Jahweh (vv. 9–11). Thirdly, when the people questioned among themselves what the substance on the ground was, Moses identified it as the promised bread and told them to gather an omer per person for the daily ration. Fourthly, when the supply of the manna remarkably doubled on the sixth day, Moses indicated that the abundance was to provide for the sabbath when no work should be done. Miraculously, the manna which spoiled if kept overnight during the week was preserved during the night of the sixth day; and equally remarkable is the notation that on the sabbath no manna was discoverable on the ground (vv. 21–24). And, finally, Moses carried out the divine command to preserve an omer of manna as a memorial (vv. 32–34).

The narrative presents and is intended to convey in religious language the involvement of Jahweh in his people's welfare. There is little rebuke for the grumbling people. Israel was young (Hos. 11:1); Jahweh was patient. The severity of the sabbath command (as exemplified in Num. 15:32 ff.) is quite foreign to the casual attitude some Israelites apparently displayed (16:27). The sabbath observance is interwoven in the narrative of the manna much as the Feast of Unleavened Bread became part of the Passover liturgy. It seems to suggest that the sabbath was an innovation which Moses sought to establish.

Comparable parallels to the curative tree and the manna have not proved altogether satisfactory. Rosenmüller adduced from the practices of the Tamils and Peruvians some analogies to the sweetening of the water by the tree wood, and August Dillmann suggests that "there might be a bush or tree, whose leaves, fruit, bark or wood were able to sweeten bitter water" (cp. 2 Kings 2:19 ff.). Jesus ben Sirach (ca. 180 B.C.) supports this general position.

> The Lord created medicines from the earth,
>   and a sensible man will not despise them.
> Was not water made sweet with a tree
>   in order that his power might be known? (38:4–5).

But beyond some vague resemblances much remains unanswered. The same is much more the case when an historical counterpart is sought for the manna.

Manna (Hebrew, *man*) was apparently unrecognized by Israel because when they saw the substance, they said to one another, "What is it (Heb., *man hû*)?" Moses, experienced in the desert region of Sinai, identified the material as bread. It appeared to fall as rain from heaven (v. 4), and when the dew lifted over the surface of the wilderness, there was a fine, flaky substance, as fine as frost, on the ground (vv. 14–16). It was like coriander seed, a flavoring spice; it had the appearance of bdellium, a gum resin from various trees of the genus *Commiphora* used for its aromatic qualities. The manna tasted like cakes baked with oil and was gathered to be ground, boiled in pots, and baked thereafter in cakes (Ex. 16:23; Num. 11:7–9; cp. Ps. 78:24, where it is called "the grain of heaven"). The substance appeared on the desert floor in the early morning, but melted in the heat of the sun (v. 21) and spoiled if kept overnight (vv. 19–20,24). The manna was available in abundant supply, enough to provide each individual well with a daily ration amounting to some two quarts (v. 16 ff., 32 f., 36). Manna was an integral part of the diet of Israel during their sojourn in the wilderness and ceased when they entered the land of Canaan (Ex. 16:35; Josh. 5:12). Apparently the phenomenon belonged to the Peninsula of Sinai.

Historical counterparts to the manna of Sinai have been sought in exudations from trees or bushes, in excretions from insects, and other dubious productions, but it is fair to say that nothing that has been adduced fits the description in any great detail. This is not to decry the parallels suggested; these serve to illustrate the means Jahweh may have chosen. Part of the problem is in our ignorance of the ancient dietary patterns and the foodstuffs of Sinai of three thousand years removed; part is the vast differences existing in the mentality of the Hebrew source and our incoordinate facilities to understand. Whatever the difficulties be, the essential matter is clear: Jahweh provided for his people in the forbidding wilderness of Sinai, nourished and nurtured them to serve his universal purpose.

It may be candidly admitted that the new experiences were exceedingly trying for Israel. Their impoverished diet is almost inconceivable to a modern American. An analogous situation of the abundant food resources available to Israel in Egypt and the subsistence level diet to which they were now reduced is provided by T. E. Lawrence in writing of the veteran traveler C. H. Doughty. Doughty had been brought up in England with its rich and plentiful food and moderate climate, but he had identified himself with the nomads of Arabia Deserta, shared their inhospitable climate and lean hospitality, subsisted on a diet of camel milk, rare meals of dates or meat, and minimal other foodstuffs—a diet which spelled starvation for an Englishman.[7] Yet added to this were the marches across rocky and toilsome country, under a burning sun or in keen exhausting winds. Reason, then, may mitigate the exasperation of the people in their precarious plight, at least, censure any conjured-up criticism of a well-fed modern man.

The later pious might sing that Israel had a mountaintop experience when

> He commanded the skies above,
>   and opened the doors of heaven;
> and he rained down upon them manna to eat,
>   and gave them the grain of heaven.
> Man ate of the bread of angels;
>   he sent them food in abundance. (Ps. 78:23–25).

Whether the bread came from heaven or not, the embittered people later had substantially less appreciation. The outcries of the discouraged people were met with gentle forbearance. Israel was young, capable of youthful misjudgments, but Israel was a son and ever loved. "When Israel was young, I loved him, and out of Egypt I called my son" (Hosea 11:1). However, when complaining became a way of life and the climate where other malevolence spawned, sterner measures were indicated.

On the other hand, the quails afford an analogy to the known migratory pattern of the partridge in their northern or southern flight from Arabia to Europe. In enormous numbers they fly with the wind (cf. Num. 11:31), settle for the night quite exhausted, and can be captured without difficulty.

3. At Rephidim (Ex. 17). The introductory verse indicates that the more than two hundred miles Israel had traveled on the east side of the sea was not a continuing march but a trek punctuated with encampments. The desert terrain which they traversed was arid and waterless; marches had to be made consonant with anticipated water resources. At Rephidim their water supply had become exhausted and with it the patience of the people. In their thirst they quarreled (Heb., *rib)* with Moses (vv. 2–4) and put Jahweh to the trial (Heb., *nasa),* asking, "Is Jahweh present with us or not?" Again confronted by the people's hostility, Moses was instructed to smite with his rod on the rock at Horeb; and when he had done so, the waters flowed from the rock. The unpleasantness of the altercation dubbed the name of the place Massah (from Hebrew *nasa)*, meaning "trial," and Meribah (from Hebrew *rib; me* is but a prefix; the Heb. *ah,* a suffix), meaning "quarrel" (cp. Deut. 6:16; Ps. 81:7; 95:8 f., and the similar situation in Num. 20:12; Ps. 106:32 f.).

If thirst and hunger were not enough, the predatory Amalekites, a roving nomadic people of the desert, threatened the people at Rephidim. Their heartless foray is described in Deuteronomy 25:17–19. "Remember what Amalek did to you on the way as you came out of Egypt, how he attacked you on the way, when you were faint and weary, and cut off at your rear all who lagged behind you; and he did not fear God." The last sentence is particularly ominous and indicates the heartless cruelty of the raid.

Here, for the first time, the existence of the people was threatened by war. In Egypt they had been protected by the imperial army; now they were on their own. It was a critical moment; there was a well-founded fear that Israel was unfit for combat (13:17). Nevertheless, Moses organized a resistance force under the command of Joshua and effectively repelled the Amalekites. The role Moses played in the fray illustrates the Israelitic concept of war as being won or lost in the higher arena and the combatants as pawns in the battle. The engagement was important in that it indicated that Israel's future would be challenged polemically by her foes, but that Israel had adequacy to overcome. The dastardly attack of Amalek demanded a righteous redress, and Moses evolved such a military policy for the future with appropriate ceremony and affirmation (vv. 14–16).

4. Jethro's Visit with Moses (Ex. 18). Tidings of Israel's release from Egypt had reached the land of Midian and the relatives of Moses. It was there that he had become a member of the family of Jethro, the priest of Midian, and had married Zipporah his daughter who presented him with two sons, Gershom and Eliezer. Jethro now set out with the family of Moses to reunite the family and to celebrate the momentous achievements.

Moses had sent his family back to the home of Jethro in Horeb for their own protection during the stormy days of his conflict with the Egyptian power (cp. Ex. 4:18 ff. with 18:2). After this separation the reunion proved to be of great joy. It was climaxed in sacrificial offerings with Jethro as celebrant and the elders of Israel sharing the sacred feast (18:7–12). The following day Jethro observed the impossible schedule Moses had as he attempted to administer justice to the people. Moses defended his practice by pointing out that "the people come to me to inquire of God; when they have a dispute, they come to me and I decide between a man and his neighbor, and I make them know the statutes of God and his decisions" (v. 17). With this his father-in-law did not disagree; his suggestion was that the program was insufferable for one man and should be shared. He proposed that a judiciary be established on five varying levels and the people were to be divided into thousands, the thousands into hundreds, the hundreds into fifties, and the fifties into tens. Over each of these divisions able, trustworthy, and unvendible rulers were to be placed who would adjudicate the complaints within their jurisdiction. Appeal could be made to the higher courts and ultimately to the supreme tribunal over which Moses himself would preside. This suggestion of Jethro was adopted and practiced.

Critics have alleged that Jethro, the father-in-law of Moses, played a very significant part in the religious development of Israel. They point out that he was the "priest of Midian," that "the mount of God" (Horeb/Sinai) was near his home, that he rejoiced to hear the superiority of Jahweh (18:11), and offered sacrifice to God (=Jahweh) in an Israelitic setting. All this is certainly admissible, but when it is suggested that Moses learned of Jahweh from his father-in-law Jethro and introduced him into the religion of Israel, the evidence is extremely tenuous. The fact that the Kenites, a Midianite clan, appear later as Jahwists does not affect the case. There are so many breaks in the scant information we have about Jethro and his religious affiliation with Moses; everything we do know regarding this period points consistently to Moses as the receptor of patriarchal religion and the formulator of the Jahwistic faith of the people of Israel. The profound impression of Moses upon Israel is singularly dominant not only in this section (Ex. 18:15 f.,

20), but throughout the Old Testament.

Theological Reflections. The exhilaration of the triumph at the Sea slowly dissipated as Israel began its arduous trek southward into the foreboding regions of Sinai. The account revolves around five themes: the cloud, the manna (and the quail), the water, and Amalek. Its purpose was not to extol the pioneers venturing as they went the unknown ways, but to exhibit the kindly providence of Jahweh.

The Cloud. It seems fair to regard the symbolic cloud as a single entity (Ex. 13:21 f.; 14:19–20,24; 16:10; 19:9,16; 24:15 f.,18; 34:5; 40:34–38) and to view the phenomenon as an expression of the presence, protection, guidance, and revelation of Jahweh.

The cloud became a symbol of hope for the exiles in Babylon as they viewed its role in the wilderness experience and claimed the same for their days.

> A voice cries,
> "In the wilderness prepare the way of Jahweh;
> make straight in the desert a highway for our God.
> Every valley shall be raised,
> and every mountain and hill be lowered;
> the uneven ground will be levelled,
> and the rough terrain a plain
> And the glory of the LORD [Ex. 16:10] shall be revealed,
> and all flesh shall see it together,
> for the mouth of Jahweh has spoken" (Isa. 40:3–5).

The symbol of the cloud is taken into the eschatology of Israel to convey the ultimate blessedness of Jahweh's presence and protection.

> Then Jahweh will create over the whole of the site of Mount Zion and over her assemblies a cloud by day, and smoke and the shining of a flaming fire by night; for over all the glory there will be a canopy and a pavilion. It will be for a shade by day from the heat, and for a refuge and a shelter from the storm and rain (Isa. 4:5 f.).

It is beautifully recast in a Christian hymn by John Newton:

> Round each habitation hovering,

See the cloud and fire appear
For a glory and a covering,
Showing that the Lord is near!

In his first letter to the Corinthians Paul reinterprets the cloud in Christian concepts. "I want you to know, brethren, that our fathers were all under the cloud, and all passed through the sea, and all were baptized into Moses in the cloud and in the sea" (1 Cor. 10:1 f.). What was valid in the days of Moses is true in a higher sense today. If the Israelites were protected by the divine presence in the cloud, we, too, share the same sheltering Presence. If they were baptized in relationship to Moses as their leader both in the cloud and in the sea, we, too, have been baptized in relationship to one greater than Moses and in a context of divine revelation and baptismal waters. One cannot but feel that our Lord had the cloud in mind when he said: "I am the light of the world; he who follows me will not walk in darkness, but will have the light of life" (John 8:12). The symbol of the cloud conveys to the Christian mind the assurance that there is an abiding presence in our midst, a protection against our foes, a revelation to chart our course, guidance for our days, and religion attested by our God.

The Manna (and the Quails). The incident of the quails (Ex. 16:3,8,12 f.) is overshadowed by the importance of the manna; nevertheless, it adds its testimony to the divine concern for the welfare of his people. The manna (Ex. 16:1–7, 12–36) became the point of departure for the discourse of Jesus on the bread of life (John 6:25–59).

When the people next saw Jesus after the feeding of the five thousand, he bade them be concerned for the food which endured to eternal life, food which the Son of man could provide. The crowd objected to his demand that they believe in him, pointing out that for forty years their fathers had eaten manna in the wilderness. Jesus countered with the assertion that Moses did not give his people the true bread from heaven, for that bread gives life to its eater. Frankly puzzled by his words, the crowd besought him to give them this type of bread. His answer was that he was the bread of life, eternally satisfying. Again the people murmured at his words and drew this response: "I am the bread of life. Your fathers ate the manna in the wilderness, and they died. This is the bread which comes down from heaven, that a man may eat of it and not die. . . . and the bread I shall give for the life of the world is my flesh" (John 6:48–51). Again the Jews took exception to his words, but he insisted that life was utterly dependent upon eating his flesh and drinking his blood. All who so participated were one with the living God, possessed of eternal life, and assured of the resurrection (vv. 52–58). Space forbids further examination save this comment,[8] that it would be good for the western church with its view of salvation largely dominated by the forensic idea of justification by faith to add to that concept the equally important idea of the mystical union of Christ and his people and of the embodiment of the divine resources by a faith participation (cp. vv. 53–57).

In Paul's letters he referred to the manna twice. In 1 Corinthians 10:3 he noted that the Christian, like the fathers in the wilderness, partakes of supernatural food to sustain him in the journey. In 2 Corinthians 8:15 he advocated that the church members contribute according to their several abilities so that equality may exist. He fortified this injunction with a quotation from Exodus 16:18: "He that gathered much had nothing over, and he that gathered little had no lack."

The Water. Water from the smitten rock (Ex. 17:1–7) in the arid wilderness brought refreshment and joy to a thirsty people. It was characteristic of Jahweh to provide for his people in their dire needs.

> He cleft rocks in the wilderness,
> and gave them drink abundantly as from the deep.
> He made streams come out of the rock,
> and caused waters to flow down like rivers
> (Ps. 78:15–16).

Such an event prompted the oracle to the Babylonian exiles with the assurance that their long march back to Palestine would not be without divine solicitation.

They thirsted not when he led them forth
through the deserts;
he made water flow for them from the rock;
he cleft the rock and the waters gushed out (Isa. 48:21).

Would Jahweh, then, do less for them? No, indeed!

I will open rivers on the bare heights,
and fountains in the midst of the valleys;
I will make the wilderness a pool of water,
and the dry land springs of water (Isa. 41:18).

Interpreting the Exodus incident in Christian terms, Paul indicated that all the Jewish fathers drank the same supernatural drink, for they drank from the supernatural Rock which followed them, and the Rock was Christ (1 Cor. 10:4 f.). Following a Jewish tradition that the water-producing rock accompanied the people in their wilderness journey, the apostle draws the analogy that the Christian is amply provided with the water (of life; cp. John 4:14; 7:37; Rev. 21:6; 22:1,17).

See the streams of living waters,
Springing from eternal love,
Well supply thy sons and daughters,
And all fear of want remove;

Who can faint, while such a river
Ever flows their thirst t' assuage?
Grace, which, like the Lord, the giver,
Never fails from age to age.
—John Newton

Amalek (Ex. 17:8–16). The dastardly raid of Amalek on Israel provided an example of gross international injustice. Accordingly, it was enshrined in a book of remembrance and affirmed in sacrifice that such crime must be punished and to that end the nation dedicated itself. It is not unlike the international immorality that the prophets censure and condemn (Amos 1). Wherever injustice prevails, wherever tyranny despoils, wherever humanity bleeds there must the church's hand be lifted up in protest till wounds heal, till tyrants cease, till justice prevails.

NOTES

[1] On the problem of numbers in the Old Testament see the conservative but judicious remarks of R.A.H. Gunner in his article entitled "Number," particularly Section II in *The New Bible Dictionary*, edited by J. D. Douglas. Grand Rapids, Eerdmans, 1962.

[2] Compare this with the full itinerary in Numbers 33.

[3] Compare the direction of the winds in Psalm 78:26.

[4] It was given this name in retrospect, but was fully operational long before the Philistines arrived in Palestine (about twelfth century B.C.)

[5] Compare Psalms 78:52 f.; 81:5b,6; 105:37 f., 106:8–12; 114:1, 3*a*,5*a*; 136:13–15.

[6] *The Suez Canal: Notes and Statistics.* Copyright 1952 in England by the Compagnie Universelle du Canal Maritime de Suez, 1952, p. 7.

[7] C. H. Doughty, *Travels in Arabia Deserta.* New York: Boni & Liverright (1921). Introduction, p. xviii.

[8] Israel was the son of God (Ex. 4:22 f.; Hos. 11:1), was tried by lack of food (Ex. 17:3), and miserably failed in the trial (Deut. 8:3). Jesus is the Son of God (Matt. 3:17), was tried by lack of food (Matt. 4:2), but triumphed in the trial (Matt. 4:3 f.; Heb. 5:8).

IV

The Covenant at Sinai

(19—24)

A. Its Theophany (19:3–25)

These chapters are among the most important in the Old Testament and are basic for an understanding of the concept of covenant. Their setting is immediately presented (19:1–2). Three months after Israel departed from Egypt, the people arrived at Mount Sinai. It was a short trek from Rephidim, following the inland defiles of the Wilderness of Sin southeastwardly to the Wilderness of Sinai and to their encampment in the plain before the mount where they were to remain almost a year (Num. 10:11). It is quite likely that the wide valley of *er-Raha*, some two miles long and one-third to two-thirds of a mile wide, became the site of their new location. Fronting the plain rise three majestic mountain peaks: *Ras-es-Safsah* to the northwest, *Jebel Musa* (Arabic: "the mount of Moses"), and *Jebel Katarin*. The traditional identification of Mount Sinai has been with *Jebel Musa*, some 7,363 feet in height, which towers over the plain like a mighty pulpit. Here sequestered in this remote and solitary region, with its massive mountainous grandeur and expansive vistas of arresting greatness, Israel was to have its rendezvous with Jahweh, an event which would profoundly affect the history of the world. It was a setting worthy of the solemn event.

Sinai had been the scene of Jahweh's revelation to Moses in the burning bush (Ex. 3). Apparently, the mountain Horeb/Sinai had anterior religious associations since it is referred to as "the mountain of God" (Ex. 3:1; 18:5); and in the call narrative of Moses it is singled out to become the place where he would one day lead the oppressed Israelites (3:12).

1. The Basic Provisions of the Covenant (19:4–6). Once encamped before the mount, Moses went up to God, and "Jahweh called to him out of the mount"—eerie words indeed!—and enunciated the overarching provisions of a covenant to be entered into by himself and Israel. The text of the oracle begins with a short preamble to set the tone of the transaction (v. 4). The mighty deeds of Jahweh in the defeat of the Egyptians and in the liberation of Israel are norms which will provide the tone for the covenant. In this charged context Israel must contribute obedience and fidelity to Jahweh while Jahweh will accord Israel the status of a people for his own possession, a kingdom of priests, and a holy nation (vv. 5 f.).

These stipulations of the covenantal oracle (vv. 4–6) must needs be set against their proper background. The ultimate purpose in the contract is the welfare of all men, a deduction that is apparent from the words: "for all the earth is mine" (v.5; cp.9:29). The Lord of all the earth is concerned for the total race (cp. Gen. 12:3). The covenant, then, cannot be interpreted with any suggestion of favoritism or partiality—a truth Israel often forgot (Amos 3:2; 9:7). To effect the good of all, Jahweh deigned to select a moral people ("If you will obey my voice and keep my covenant") who would conform to his will and to whom he might entrust his universal program of salvation (cp. Ex. 9:16). The pattern of obedience and fidelity is more fully presented in the ensuing Decalogue and covenantal code (Ex. 20—23). In language reminiscent of Exodus 6:6 ff., Jeremiah underscores the bounden responsibilities of the people to obey the commandment of Jahweh in order to validate the covenant.

> You shall say to them, Thus says Jahweh, the God of Israel: Cursed be the man who does not heed the words of this covenant which I commanded your fathers when I brought them out of the land of Egypt, from the iron furnace, saying, Listen to my voice, and do all that I command you. So shall you be my people, and I will be your God, that I may perform the oath which I swore to your fathers, to give them a land flowing with milk and honey, as at this day. (Jer. 11:3–5)

> Thus says Jahweh of hosts, the God of Israel: Add your burnt offerings to your sacrifices, and eat the flesh. For in the day that I brought them out of the land of Egypt, I did not speak to your fathers or command them concerning burnt offerings and sacrifices. But this command I gave them,

Obey my voice and I will be your God and you shall be my people, and walk in all the way that I command you (Jer. 7:21–23; cp. Jer. 24:8)

The purpose of Jahweh for Israel would assume the form of a ministering priesthood under Jahweh the king ("a kingdom of priests") and a consecrated people ("a holy nation"). It was a breathtaking proposal, to become "a people for his own possession," peculiarly related to God in the redemption of the world.

The covenant here envisaged is the reiteration in national terms of the patriarchal covenant, a restatement of those basic contractual stipulations relating them to the contemporary situation. Israel was to be the high priest of the nations, fulfilling the impressive portrait of Abraham's priestly intercession before the God of the whole world for the salvation of the wicked cities of the plain (Gen. 18:22–32). Israel's ministry is elsewhere interpreted as the role of the suffering servant whose task is to evangelize the world (Isa. 40—55), a ministry that was fulfilled in depth in the sufferings endured for God's sake and described so eloquently in Hebrews 11:35 to 12:1.

After the majestic plans of Jahweh had been revealed, Moses returned to the camp and communicated them to the elders of the people. The people consented to the divine program and pledged their obedience. Immediately thereafter Moses ascended the mount for his second audience with Jahweh and reported the words of the people. It is quite moving to witness Moses bringing the answer of his people to an omniscient God and climbing the rugged mountain for more than three hours to gain that engagement!

Two additional matters are then introduced: Jahweh will approach Moses in a thick cloud in the audience of the people so that they may have their faith confirmed in him; and the people are to prepare themselves ritualistically for the divine event. More particularly, they are to bathe, assume clean clothing, abstain from sexual relations, and eschew any approach to the mount where Jahweh is to appear (vv. 10–15; cp. 21–24).

The underlying ideas of the ritualistic prescriptions (vv. 10:14,22,23) here are the Hebraic concept of holiness and its antithesis, impurity. Holiness is a very primitive idea, inherent in Semitic religion generally and inherited by Israel as part of its religious culture. In its earlier form holiness had nothing to do with morality or ethics. The Mesopotamian Ishtar may flail her enemies with her sword, decapitate them with sadistic delight, ride naked on her horse with blood up to its belly, and still be captioned on the icon as "the holy one"!

Israel purified the pagan notion of holiness and reinterpreted it as an expression of its own religious ideas. Holiness has been compared to "taboo" or "mana" and has been illustrated from modern science by the analogy of radioactivity.

Jahweh is the holy One, "majestic in holiness" (Ex. 15:11). Holiness is not a quality or a predicate such as righteousness; it is rather essential being. Jahweh swears by himself, by his life, by his name, and by his holiness. These four entities are synonymous and denote the individual person. Accordingly, holiness has the significance of transcendental being, the veritable nature of God, the being infinitely removed from man: separate, unique, alone.

An associative idea is that holiness is contagious. The altar is "most holy," and whatever touches it becomes holy (Ex. 29:37; 30:29; cp. Matt. 23:17,19). To be sanctified suddenly (Latin: *sanctus*=holy) from a secular or unclean state is dangerous. When Jahweh descends upon the mountain, it becomes holy. All who touch it without due precaution or authorization acquire holiness and perish (Ex. 19:11*b*–13,20–24). To prepare oneself for traffic with the holy, the individual must separate himself from the uncleanness of common life by bathing, attiring himself with *clean* (=holy) clothing, and abstaining from sexual relations, which were considered defiling. These are the ritualistic prescriptions to be observed by the people to avoid the jeopardy of death. Moreover, there are here gradations in the approachability of Jahweh even though the ritualistic precautions have been fulfilled. The people are restrained from access to Jahweh by bounds about the mountain. Should they or an animal even so much as touch the mount, that life must be destroyed because of the holiness acquired. The priests likewise are enjoined to perform the same ritualistic preparation as the people;

however, these may draw closer to Jahweh than the people (vv. 22,24). Moses and at times Aaron alone had access to the mountain, for they alone were the authorized personnel.

Holiness, as it matured in the religious experience of Israel, assumed a development along two lines. (1) The ancient notion of its fearfulness, its untoward consequences for those unprepared, and its contagious nature, were preserved largely with modifications in the priestly tradition, particularly in Leviticus, Numbers, and Ezekiel, as well as in early Judaism. Here the problem was the identification of physical entities with moral qualities. Jesus differentiated between the two when he defended himself for not having washed his hands before a meal (Mark 7:2–8; Matt. 15:1–10). The Christian faith has rejected the physical aspect of holiness. (2) In other traditions, the prophetic and psalmic, the transcendental concept of holiness was developed (cp. Isa. 6; the thrice repeated ascription of holiness to Jahweh is tantamount to infinite holiness, holiness to the *n*th degree). Jahweh is identified with his purposes in history as "the holy One *of Israel*" (Isa. 1:4; 5:24). Holiness is ethicized: "the Holy God shows himself holy *in righteousness*" (Isa. 5:16). That is, when the essence of God flows into history, it assumes the recognizable characteristics of morality, much as light passing through a prism results in the spectrum.

Another basic term in this block of materials is *covenant*. This term (Hebrew: *berith*) is used in the Old Testament to denote a compact or agreement made between two parties. In its fullest form the covenanting parties recite the terms of the agreement, assume the obligations of a binding oath, shake hands with one another (betokening the unity achieved thereby and the troth pledged), pass between the severed sacrificial animal sacramentalizing the agreement, and imprecate maledictions on him who violates the covenant (compare Jer. 11:3; Deut. 27:11 ff.; 28:15 ff.). These details can be gleaned from the various covenants described in the Old Testament, particularly that which is portrayed in the dream experience of Abram (Gen. 15:7–21, in which Jahweh assumes the symbolism of fire; cp. Jer. 34:10 ff.). The compacts consummated between God and the patriarchs are heavily underlined in the traditions (Gen.

15:18; 17:2 ff.; Ex. 2:24; 6:4 f.). The event at Sinai is the restatement of the patriarchal covenants in contemporary terms (Ex. 19:5; 24:7–8). The parties to the agreement, the stipulations agreed upon (Ex. 19:5 f.,8,20–24), and the sacrament of the covenant (Ex. 24) are fully represented.

2. *Encounter with the Holy One.* The theophany of Jahweh on Mount Sinai is one of the most impressive appearances of God in the Old Testament. Jahweh announced that he would come in a symbolism of the thick cloud and communicate with Moses (v. 9). The mountain was to be sealed off from the people and animals on pain of death; to touch the holy mountain would be fatal, though one notices that the victim was to be stoned or shot with an arrow by the people (vv. 12 ff.). On the morning of the descent of Jahweh, thunders and lightnings together with a thick cloud appeared upon the mountain (v. 16). The trumpet, with a very loud and sustained blast, sounded increasingly while the mount was wrapped in smoke, because Jahweh descended upon it in fire; and the smoke of it ascended like the smoke of a kiln; and the whole mountain quaked (v. 18 f.). This fearful advent caused the people to tremble and to retreat afar off (20:18–21).

How is one to interpret this awesome event? There are three interpretations which deserve to come under review.

(1) The literalistic view approaches the problem of the descent of Jahweh upon Mount Sinai and the giving of the law with the understanding that all is actual history. The book of Deuteronomy adds many references to the narrative (4:11 f.,15,24,33,36; 5:2–5,22–28; 9:3,10,15,21; 10:4; 18:16). Interestingly, the Greek translation of Deuteronomy 33:2 is to the effect that the Lord was accompanied by myriads of his holy ones, who in the parallelism of the verse are identified with his angels at his right hand. This is the basis of the idea that the law was ordained by angels through an intermediary (Moses; Gal. 3:19). The allegorical mode of interpreting the Scriptures became dominant in the early church so that the problem of literalism was not examined to any great degree because it did not constitute the essential meaning of the Scriptures. Where such problems were discovered, they were dismissed quite summarily.

Martin Buber feels, as we all do, the merciless problem of truth, but admits that if we assume the events as actual scientific history, Moses becomes a stranger to our world. "The words of the covenant . . . could surely not have entered the world thus, in such optical and acoustical pomp and circumstance; and where the narrative reports them as having been written on Tables of Stone—things happen quite differently, in silence and solitude.[1]

(2) The method that the modern historical school has advocated views the events of Sinai as having some historical foundation. "It is highly probable that in the locality where the events are placed, there really occurred natural phenomena which are reflected in the narrative" (Dillmann). No matter how we check and test the account, no basis will be found for doubting the essential historicity of what is described as having happened. Nevertheless, "every attempt to penetrate to some factual process which is concealed behind the awe-inspiring picture is quite in vain. We are no longer in a position to replace that immense image by actual data" (Buber). It is suggested quite reasonably that the natural foundation of the description of Exodus 19:16,18 (see 20:18) is evidently a thunderstorm; and like so many parallel places in the prophets and psalms, it must be viewed symbolically. A graphic analogy is afforded by Psalm 18 (2 Samuel 22) wherein a king (v. 50; cp. vv. 43 ff.,47 f.) recounts the divine succour he received in battle when he was hopelessly surrounded by his mortal foes. He was assured that the invisible God had entered the lists with his awesome might and, all unseen, turned the tide of the battle to rescue his servant (cp. Ps. 77:19), but how could he communicate this intervention of God in the available resources of language? He chose a physical category and used it as a symbol of the unseen and metaphysical. He selected one of the most overwhelming phenomena of the natural world, one replete with *mysterium tremens* and universally meaningful: the awe-inspiring thunderstorm. In the symbolism of a fearful storm he portrays the advent of God into his situation. All the accouterments are pressed into service: the reverberation of the thunder (v. 7), the clouds (smoke) and lightning bolts (v. 8), the swift wind (v. 10), the thick clouds dark with water (v. 11), hail, and thunder (vv. 12 ff.).

Jahweh was not the storm itself; the storm was the element, the regalia, the means to realize his purpose. Such a presentation is called a theophany ("an appearance of God"), presented here in the symbolism of a devastating storm. This literary procedure is used by the prophets to describe Jahweh's invasion of history and its judgment (Hab. 3:3 ff; Mic. 1:3 f.; cp. also Ps. 68:7 f.; Judg. 5:4 f.). The theophany of Jahweh at Sinai is not different; it includes in its description "thunders and lightnings, a thick cloud upon the mount" (vv. 9,16). In Exodus 19:18 the descent of Jahweh upon Sinai is in fire, with smoke going up like the smoke of a kiln. The narrative (like Ps. 18 and Hab. 3) is to be conceived as a dramatic picture, the details of which are not to be pressed. Israel is attempting in this tradition to convey an overwhelming religious reality and employs the only means available to communicate abstract truth, through symbolism and impressionism.

Professor William Sanday to whom the church is indebted for his profound and reverent scholarship suggested that

> When the Decalogue is prefaced, "God spake these words and said," nothing could be more natural than that the words should be represented as coming out of the storm, with "thunders and lightnings, and a thick cloud upon the mount, and the voice of a trumpet exceeding loud" (Exod. xix.16). And again when we remember how, in the covenant of God with Abraham, the Divine presence is represented by a "smoking furnace and a flaming torch that passed between" the pieces of the victims, we are not surprised when we read that "Mount Sinai was altogether in smoke, because the Lord descended upon it in fire; and the smoke thereof ascended as the smoke of a furnace" (ver. 18). These are just poetic accessories, emblematic of the central fact that the words proceeded from God. The literal truth was that God spoke to the heart of Moses: the poetic truth was that He spoke in thunder and lightning from the crest of Sinai.[2]

To the same effect are the words of one of the greatest of all Old Testament scholars, Franz Delitzsch: "It was in the soul of Moses that the Divine thoughts of the Decalogue found their expression in language; the human words in which God's revelation is here cast are words of Moses."[3]

(3) The third interpretation is the cultic approach. The historical school had discounted much of the numinous element inherent in

the traditions of Israel, festival, ritual, locale, and personnel. In Exodus 1—19, before the tabernacle was in operation and the law given, there were purification rites, a proto-passover observance, a tent of meeting, the testimony of the ark, sacrifices, oracles, priesthood, circumcision, and the mount of God. W. Beyerlin believes that the cult of Israel was the dominant influence in shaping the Sinai tradition and postulates a recurring festival of covenant renewal in early Israel as its setting in life. He argues that the motif of the sound of the trumpet (Ex. 19:13,16,19; 20:18) corresponds to the cultic announcement of the epiphany of God (Ps. 47:6; 68:18 f.); the cloud of smoke has its parallels in an incense rite (though this is doubtful); and the cultic entities mentioned above have their counterparts in the religion of Israel. It is, therefore, to the cultic recitation of the tradition (Deut. 26:5–11) that one must look to see the antecedents of Israel's experience at the mount (cp. Deut. 26:5–11; Ex. 10:2; 12:26 f.; 13:8 f.; Gen. 18:19). But while there are some suggestive ideas in the cultic attempt to reconstruct the actual events (indeed, even the very conservative C. F. Keil believes that the cloudy pillar may have withdrawn itself to the mountain and hence be the source of the theophany in fire), it is doubtful whether the cultic approach has an adequate basis to interpret all the data.

In the realm of religion the letter kills, but the spirit gives life (2 Cor. 3:16). To know Christ after the flesh, that is, to be acquainted only with the physical surroundings of his life, is to miss the essential meaning of the Christ who must be known spiritually (2 Cor. 5:16). The words that Jesus spoke were spirit and were life (John 6:63); the flesh profited nothing. Whatever view we may espouse, it should be the one that brings the essential significance into clearest focus.

Whenever Josephus, the renowned Jewish historian (c. 37–c. 100), dealt with anything capable of various interpretations, he gave the sage advice that each of his readers should judge the matter as it appeared to him (*Antiquities* i:108; ii:348; iii:81). Augustine brings the matter more sharply into focus when he writes: "In the study of the various matters of creation one should not exercise a vain and perishing curosity, but ascend toward what is immortal and everlasting" (*De vera religione*, XXIX). Martin Buber admirably sums up the problem:

> What takes place here is a meeting between two fires, the earthly and the heavenly; and if either of them is struck out, there is an immediate lacuna in the picture which has so enraptured the generations of the People of Israel and the generations of the Christian peoples.[4]

Theological Reflections. The imperishable truths enunciated in Exodus 19 are based on the premises that Jahweh is the Creator of the world and that his purposes involve all mankind ("for all the earth is mine" v. 5). Israel is his selected agent to minister the knowledge of God to all. As a ministering community ("a kingdom of priests" v. 6) the nation must be separated, dedicated, and morally adequate to fulfill its role as the high priest of the nations. Jahweh is transcendent, without form, fearful in holiness, yet concerned to reveal himself, condescending to use human mores and make them symbolic of deeper and profounder spiritual truth. The trappings of the theophany have overtones beyond the physical where their true meaning is ultimately to be found. The impression created by the theophany is one for the soul, the inward consciousness of man's deepest reach.

The preamble of the covenant (19:5) is applied directly to the church in 1 Peter 2:9: "You are a chosen race, a royal priesthood, a holy nation, God's own people" . . . The author then adds in the words of Isaiah 43:21 the purpose to which this community is dedicated: ". . . that you may declare the wonderful deeds of him who called you out of darkness into his marvelous light."

It should be carefully noted that the preamble begins with the words: "If you will obey my voice and keep my covenant" (v. 5). The high privileges are restricted by the requirement of fidelity. If the conditional clause is negated and the community does not obey the voice of Jahweh and keep his covenant, then the covenant is null and void. The election of Israel was a moral election, a selection that involved a moral articulation; when the nation refused obedience and became immoral, it ceased to be the people of God. Hosea announces this sad eventuality to the northern kingdom; Jahweh has divorced Israel: "You are not my people and I am not your God" (1:9). A moral and obedient remnant qualified for the promises; the immoral and disobedient nation was lost in the Assyrian sands.

The epistle to the Hebrews contrasts the assembly of Israel met before Mount Sinai to witness the awesome theophany and there to conclude the old covenant with the assembly of Christians who have entered into the new covenant.

> Remember where you stand: not before the palpable, blazing fire of Sinai, with the darkness, gloom, and whirlwind, the trumpet-blast and the oracular voice, which they heard, and begged to hear no more; for they could not bear the command, If even an animal touches the mountain, it must be stoned. So appalling was the sight, that Moses said, I shudder with fear.
>
> No, you stand before Mount Zion and the city of the living God, heavenly Jerusalem, before the myriads of angels, the full concourse and assembly of the first-born citizens of heaven, and God the judge of all, and the spirits of good men made perfect, and Jesus the mediator of a new covenant, whose sprinkled blood has better things to tell than the blood of Abel (Heb. 12:18–24, NEB).

Since the Christian has the higher privileges bestowed upon him, he ought so much the more to hear the voice that speaks (v. 25).

B. Its Principles (20—23)

The principles of the covenant are contained in the Decalogue (20:1–17) and the covenant code or common law (chs. 21—23). A word of introduction is necessary in order to appreciate this important segment of the Sinaitic covenant.

The history of law assumes to a large extent the societal pattern of the group. In early tribal society the paterfamilias or sheik regulated his domain by practical mores which experience had proved worthy patterns of behavior. These mores were epitomized in maxims or proverbs, succinct distillation of proven experience which set the pattern of normative behavior. Law, therefore, has its roots in proverbial wisdom sayings.

The ancient Near East has dozens of collections of this type of proverbial literature, both in Egypt and in Mesopotamia, with antecedents reaching back into the third millennium B.C. They assume the form of a testament in which a father imparts to his son the results of his experience in life. Later, when education was transferred to teachers, the teachers were called fathers, and the pupils, sons. In presenting the words of wisdom to his son or pupil, the father enforced the injunction for the particular mores by some motivating reason.

> You shall take no bribe,
> for a bribe blinds the officials
> and subverts the cause of the just.
> (Ex. 23:8)

The first line provides the norm to be followed; lines two and three encourage or motivate the performance by some valid reason and are accordingly called motivation clauses.

When society lost its familial pattern, became depersonalized, and moved into national dimensions, the law gradually lost its paternalism so that in the later law the motivation clauses are increasingly suppressed. In the Old Testament, however, the transition from the proverb saying with motivation clause to purely legal statute is quite observable. While wisdom literature and law developed their own particularities in the later development, the laws in Exodus 20—23 still betray some evidence of the transitional phase. This may be easily demonstrated if the several laws regarding the cursing of one's parents (Ex. 23:17; Lev. 20:9; Deut. 27:16) are compared with their proverbial counterparts (Prov. 20:20; 28:24; 30:17). In addition to testamentary admonitions or instructions, the ancient Near East produced codifications of law, such as the Lipit-Ishtar Law Code (ca. 1875 B.C.); the fragmentary code in the time of Ur Nammu of Ur (ca. 2050 B.C.); the laws of Eshnunna (ca. 1830–1817 B.C.), the Code of Hammurabi (1728–1686 B.C.), the Middle Assyrian Laws (twelfth century B.C.), the Neo-Babylonian Laws (sixth century B.C.), and the Hittite Laws (thirteenth century B.C.). In addition to the law codes, jurisprudential documents with their interpretation of the law in specific cases have been recovered in Mesopotamia and in Egypt. With these various codes originating from different linguistic groups and locales as well as from different periods, it is possible to compare biblical law. It becomes quite apparent that the covenant code has many similarities to these ancient legal collections, a testimony to its antiquity and its character.

On the other hand, the Decalogue has much that is unique. Its literary pattern differs from most of the laws in Exodus 21—23. The latter laws presuppose a situation: "When men quarrel and one strikes the other with a stone or with his fist . . ." after which follows the judgment or verdict. This form of law is called *casuistic law* and is the normal pattern in which the ancient Near Eastern law is cast. By contrast, the Ten Commandments do not depend on or presuppose any contingency at all; they are cast into the intensive imperative mood without qualification. This type of law may be called *apodictic law,* a term which expresses the absolute confrontation of the law. This form is generally peculiar to Israelite law and suggests that it was not derived from Semitic law generally, but rather was an innovative Israelitic creation.

A comparative examination of the Decalogue with other ancient cultures indicates that the first four commandments are peculiarly Israelitic even though it may be admitted that some faint resemblance is encountered in the preambles to the ancient law codes. The other six commandments are naturally discovered in other cultures because of their generic character. However, whether one examine the 125th chapter of the Egyptian *Book of the Dead*—the so-called Negative Confession—or the Mesopotamian *Shurpu* incantation series with its high ethical content, he will discover nowhere the ethical grandeur of the Decalogue with comparable succinctness and incomparable religious setting.

The second major part of the legislation is the so-called covenant code proper (Ex. 21—23). Its contents include the following: slavery (21:20–21), battery (21:12–15,17–27), kidnapping (21:16), cursing of parents (21:17), negligence (21:28–36; 22:10–15), theft (22:1–4), property damage (22:5–6), seduction (22:16–17), bestiality (22:19), religious statutes (20:23–26; 22:20,28–31; 23:10–19), humane laws (22:21; 23:9; 22:22–25; 23:4–5,9), and judicial laws (23:1–3,6–8).

This corpus of law is largely casuistic in form and may be viewed in part as the common law inherited and adapted by the Israelites from contemporary culture. As such it can be remarkably paralleled by the aforementioned law codes of the ancient Near East both in form and substance. Approximately two thirds of Exodus 21—23 is generally coincident with the codes of the ancient Near Eastern laws. The remaining one third, without counterpart in the other codes, contains humane and religious prescriptions which are peculiar to Jahwism.

Growth is the law of life and the life of law. Law is essentially dynamic in nature, and because it is invoked to adjudicate every new dispute, law grows continually in breadth and depth. Every law code has discernible stratification; some laws are from time immemorial while others are palpably recent; yet both exist side by side. A body of law reflects generally the society that produced it. The letter of the law is one matter; the interpretation of the law quite another. It is the art of jurisprudence that provides the normative evaluation of the particular statute. The above factors are inherent in the formulation of Exodus 21—23. An interesting example of the use to which law was put is found in the citation of the statute regarding Hebrew slavery (Ex. 21:2) by Jeremiah the prophet, who indicts the nation for transgressing this statute.

> The word of Jahweh came to Jeremiah from Jahweh: "Thus says Jahweh, the God of Israel: I made a covenant with your fathers when I brought them out of the land of Egypt, out of the house of bondage, saying, 'At the end of six years each of you must set free the fellow Hebrew who has been sold to you and has served you six years; you must set him free from your service.' But you fathers did not listen to me or incline their ears to me" (Jer. 34:12–14).

The covenantal code tolerates slavery, permits a parent to sell his child into slavery, advocates the *lex talionis,* and regards a slave as a chattel. On the other hand, in the same code are high principles of justice, fair practices, humane expressions, and enlightened mores; and there is more of the latter qualities than the former. Israel's religious comprehension was progressive. At the beginning of her existence its contemporary and inherited culture was horizontal in structure, but with the advent of revelation vouchsafed to the patriarchs and their heirs there entered the vertical dimension of divine revelation. Immediately tensions developed. To illustrate, if Abraham were to have acted as a faithful adherent to the accepted practices that obtained in the Semitic world, he would have had to offer his son as a sacrifice. The Jahwistic revelation, the new leaven that had entered the lump, repudiated this time-honored practice for a nobler dedication (Gen. 22; Mic. 6:6–8). The institution of slavery was everywhere acceptable in the ancient world, yet in the Israelite tradition there arose a dissident voice. If God had made man in his image, and if the image of God vouchsafed to him the privilege of self-determination, was it not immoral to restrict the inalienable freedom of any man? It took many centuries to act on that great truth. If, then, there are laws which seem incongruous to us—and there are—they represent Israel's contemporary comprehension, its religious thought in the process of maturation. In their fuller and maturer realization of the mind of God, the Israelites would challenge their moral inadequacy.

The crucible where these matters were tried was within the community of the ethical. In Exodus 22:8 f. the litigant who appeared before the court is described as one coming near to God and the resulting verdict as handed down by God himself. Judges who are the vicegerents of God's judgment are actually called "gods" (Heb. *elohim*). In Exodus 18:15 f., where Moses is discussing his judiciary function with his father-in-law Jethro, he said ". . . the people come to me to inquire of God; when they have a dispute, they come to me and I decide between a man and his neighbors, and I make them know the statutes of God and his decisions." The Israelites were too worldly wise not to recognize corruption in the judiciary, but were confident in the integrity of the nation generally to believe that the courts processed divine judgments.

In the Decalogue particularly and in the covenant code may be viewed elements that have arrived, that were eternally valid, and elements that were in transition to be challenged with an ever deepening understanding of God, not unlike growth rings in the development of Israel's religious thought. The development may be witnessed if the covenant code is compared with the later and, to a large degree, parallel codes of Israelitic law in Leviticus, Numbers, and Deuteronomy. The progress is not always upward and onward for aye; there are progressions and recessions, a Hezekiah is followed by a Manasseh, but the overall view witnesses a deeper comprehension in the gentle flow of history.

The concluding portion of the covenant code (23:20–32) concerns itself with the journey to and possession of the promised land (v. 20). Jahweh pledges his blessing on national fidelity (v. 22) but threatens disaster upon disobedience (v. 21). The essential ingredients of the convenantal promises made to the patriarchs are reechoed here in the promise of the land (vv. 20,23,29), in protection (vv. 22,27 f.), and in provision (vv. 25 f.). Israel is solemnly charged to have no association either with the gods of the dwellers in Canaan (v. 24) or with its inhabitants (vv. 32 f.). Without this epilogue the covenant at Sinai would be truncated and without denouement.

Theological Reflections. Law is a small word, but a large subject. The subject may be divided here into the following general topics: the concept of the law in the Old Testament, the Pharisaic and Christian concepts of the law, and a consideration of the Ten Commandments.

The concept of the law in the Old Testament admitted more flexibility than we allow inasmuch as it consisted of religious, social, political, criminal, and civil mores formulated and venerated as law. But whatever its components, its unity was maintained. It is conceived more as an address of a personal God to Israel than an objective prescription superimposed upon a people. Law was extolled as a revelation of Jahweh, a revelation that was accompanied by enablement to fulfill the command in that it was relevant to the situation and to the individual's strength.

> This commandment which I command you this day is not too hard for you, neither is it far off. It is not in heaven, that you should say, Who will go up for us to heaven, and bring it to us, that we may hear it and do it? Neither is it beyond the sea, that you should say, Who will go over the sea for us, and bring it to us, that we may hear it and do it? But the word is very near you; it is in your mouth and in your heart, so that you can do it. (Deut. 30:11–14).

In the Psalter there are two "torah liturgies" (Ps. 19 and 119) in which the love for the law as the way of life is warmly expressed. Psalm 19 is here included because of its important bearing on the discussion. Note the various synonyms for the law at the beginning of the first six sentences, then the descriptive adjective characterizing the law, and finally the participial clause indicating what the law accomplishes. In the last sentence two adjectives are present instead of an adjective and a participial clause, but this is characteristic of Hebrew style to avoid monotonous repetition.

The law of Jahweh	is perfect,	reviving the soul;
The testimony of Jahweh	is sure,	making wise the simple;
The precepts of Jahweh	are right,	rejoicing the heart;
The commandment of Jahweh	is pure,	enlightening the eyes;
The fear of Jahweh	is clean,	enduring for ever;
The ordinances of Jahweh	are true	and righteous altogether (Ps. 19:7–9).

The psalmist then evaluates the law as more precious than much fine gold and sweeter than the drippings of the honeycomb. As the servant of Jahweh he is warned by the law and testifies that he has found great reward in keeping it. The law was a means of communion between God and his soul, a declaration of the will of God in which the psalmist found his highest joy.

In another psalm the writer contrasts the formalism of the sacrificial cult with the immediacy of God's revelatory will within his heart.

> Burnt offering and sin offering
>   thou hast not required.
> Then I said, "Lo, I come.
>   In the roll of the book it is written (prescribed) for me.
> I delight to do thy will, O my God;
>   Thy law is within my heart. (Ps. 40:6–8).

In the New Testament nine of the Ten Commandments of the law are repeated and reaffirmed as ingredients of the Christian response (Matt 4:10; 19:18; Rom. 7:7; 13:9). Jesus admonished the rich young man with the words: "If you would enter life, keep the commandments" (Matt 19:17). The rabbis conceived the law to have 613 commandments, some 365 positive and 248 negative. No doubt with this multiplicity in mind a lawyer asked Jesus what was the great commandment in the law, to which he responded:

You shall love the Lord your God with all your heart, and with all your soul, and with all your mind. This is the great and first commandment. And a second is like it, You shall love your neighbor as yourself. On these two commandments depend all the law and the prophets (Matt. 22:37–40; cp. Rom. 13:9).

Here two precepts from the Law, Deuteronomy 6:5 and Leviticus 19:18, are united in one commandment of love and identified as the essence of the whole of the Scriptures; indeed, the basis of the Christian faith. Jesus likewise insisted that there was a certain permanency about the law, as may be gained from his words:

Think not that I have come to abolish the law and the prophets; I have come not to abolish them but to fulfil them. For truly, I say to you, till heaven and earth pass away, not an iota, not a dot, will pass from the law until all is accomplished (Matt. 5:17–18).

With this very high view of the law in mind, it comes as a shock when one first encounters some of the passages Paul wrote concerning the law. In 2 Corinthians 3:7 f. the apostle described the giving of the law in these words:

Now if the dispensation of death, carved in letters on stone, came with such splendor that the Israelites could not look at Moses' face because of its brightness, fading as this was, will not the dispensation of the Spirit be attended with greater splendor? For if there was a splendor in the dispensation of condemnation, the dispensation of righteousness must far exceed it in splendor.

In his Galatian letter Paul contrasted the old and the new covenants using Hagar the bondmaid and Sarah as allegorical figures.

Now this is an allegory: these women are two covenants. One is from Mount Sinai, bearing children for slavery; she is Hagar. Now Hagar is Mount Sinai in Arabia; she corresponds to the present Jerusalem, for she is in slavery with her children. But the Jersualem above is free, and she is our mother (Gal. 4:24–26).

In the same letter he maintained that "all who rely on works of the law are under a curse" (3:10) and that all "who would be justified by the law are severed from Christ" (5:4). Although this Pauline profile could be multiplied, a final example from his letter to the Romans must suffice:

> Now we know that whatever the law says it speaks to those who are under the law, so that every mouth may be stopped, and the whole world may be held accountable to God. For no human being will be justified in his sight by works of the law, since through the law comes knowledge of sin (3:19–20).

Now whatever the foregoing may indicate, it cannot indict Paul of disparaging the law. There are too many instances where he recognizes its divinity, its revelation, and its glory.

The resolution of the seeming incongruity in the thought of Paul must be approached from another direction. He suggests in his first letter to Timothy that the law is good, if any one uses it lawfully" (1:8), indicating that there was a right use and a wrong use of the law. The wrong use of the law may be illustrated in Paul's penetrating analysis of Pharisaic religion, an analysis with which he had had personal and empathetic identity (cp. Phil. 4 ff.; Acts 26:4 f.). In the first place, the Pharisaism Paul examines was built on an egocentric foundation. It had narcissism—that is, a complete individualism as a basis of life, an apotheosis of self, whether perceived or unperceived, and criteria for expression dictated solely by self-interest. It viewed God as an object, an individual along side of self, both separate entities, both asking and affording no quarter. The entire world beyond self had no meaning except in terms of self. When this complete self-sufficient individual entered a covenant, it was on a parity basis and regulated by reward for service rendered. But this type of individualism is inadequate in higher relationships. It spells doom for many earthly relationships, for example, in marriage two individuals become one in mystical union and therein find their true self-fulfillment in a point beyond themselves (cp. Rom. 7:1 ff.). The same obtains more fully in one's relationship to God. When a self-contained individual attempts to enter a covenant relationship with God, he discovers that he is inadequate to maintain his responsibility. The terms that God assesses are inharmonious to the individual's desire, hostile to his plans, and impossible as a means to secure the self-fulfillment his individuality projects. In a word, when such an individual seeks a relationship with God, he discovers that he is basically at enmity with God, of another mind and purpose than God's, and that the attempted relationship progressively worsens. Paul records his experience:

> What then shall we say? That the law is sin? By no means! Yet if it had not been for the law, I should not have known sin. I should not have known what it is to covet if the law had not said, "You shall not covet." But sin, finding opportunity in the commandment, wrought in me all kinds of covetousness. So the law is holy, and the commandment is holy and just and good. We know that the law is spiritual; but I am carnal sold under sin (Rom. 7:7 f.–8,12,14).

For the self-contained individual to attempt to keep the law of the covenant necessarily involves him in the curse of the covenant (Gal. 3:10 ff.) because he is morally inadequate to accept, let alone to perform his responsibility.

The utter distortion experienced by Paul in his pre-Christian experience as he attempted as a self-contained individual to keep the law, is paralleled by the same frustration and failure in the experience of others who had in common the same Pharisaic foundation of life. The Pharisees provide in their religious distortion pathetic examples of moral failure; they were proud and despised others (Luke 18:10), lovers of money (Luke 16:14), hypocritical (Matt. 23:13,15,23,25,27,29), who sought to justify themselves before men but were an abomination in the sight of God (Luke 16:15), who concentrated on trivia and were oblivious of the essentials (Matt. 23:23), and who drew from Jesus the sharpest criticism and the direst doom (Matt. 23 and parallels). This type of a self-contained religious experience rules out the possibility of divine fellowship. Jesus warned that unless one's righteousness exceeded that of the scribes and Pharisees, he would never enter the kingdom of heaven (Matt. 5:20).

When the law was given, it was given in a context of grace. It was not a compact between two individualistic entities, but more of a relationship between Creator and man, man and wife, shepherd and sheep, with mutualities bridging individualism. The confrontation of God and Israel was framed in the most interrelational terms: "I will be your God; and you will be my people" (Ex. 6:7; Jer. 31:33; Hos. 1:10). As two separate lines, made to bisect each other at right angles, transcend their individuality to become the symbol of a cross, so one's individuality must intersect the being of God, and that relationship then proves to be transcendent and definitive. That relationship is entered into by faith, a vital attachment to God in which the self-contained ground of being becomes theocentric or Christocentric, a regeneration of life that inscribes the law within the heart, absolves failure, provides fellowship, and gains true experiential knowledge of God (Heb. 8:8–12; Jer 31:31–34). When this covenantal relationship is consummated, the new being identifies with the law of God, practices the commandments, and fulfills the law. It is the advent of possibility, when the humanly impossible becomes possible through divine enablement, when men, self-contained and morally frustrated, discover life, meaning, and self-fulfillment in a faith relationship with the redemptive God. This is the reason Paul was so exercised about Peter's inconsistent behavior.

> We ourselves [said Paul] are Jews by birth and not Gentile sinners, yet who know that a man is not justified by the works of the law but through faith in Jesus Christ, even we have believed in Christ Jesus, in order to be justified by faith in Christ, and not by the works of the law, because by the works of the law shall no one be justified (Gal. 2:15 f.).

Salvation by the grace of God appropriated by man's commitment of faith becomes the dynamic of the moral life and the embodiment of the divine law in human experience.

> Do we then overthrow the law by this faith? By no means! On the contrary, we uphold the law (Rom. 3:31).

> What the law could never do, because our lower nature robbed it of all potency, God has done: by sending his own Son in a form like that of our own sinful nature, and as a sacrifice for sin, he has passed judgment against sin within that very nature, so that the commandment of the law may find fulfillment in us, whose conduct, no longer under the control of our lower nature, is directed by the Spirit (Rom. 8:3–4).

In 1 Corinthians 9:20 f., the apostle divides mankind in their relationship to the law.[5]

> To those *under* the law [*i.e.*, Israelites attempting to merit salvation by works], I became as one *under* the law—though not being myself under the law—that I might win those under the law. To those *outside* the law I became as one outside the law [i.e., the Gentiles]—not being without law toward God but *in*lawed to Christ—that I might win those *outside* the law (1 Cor. 9:20 f.).

With the law of Christ inscribed in his heart (Heb. 8:10), as the inner rector, and with the love of God poured into his heart through the Holy Spirit (Rom. 5:5) as the moral dynamic of the new life, the believer identifies with love (1 John 4:19) in its trifold expression (Matt. 19:19; 1 John 4:20). This life of love is the fulfilling of the law (Gal. 5:14; Rom. 13:8–10).

The Decalogue (Ex. 20:1–17; Deut. 5:6–21). The Ten Commandments (Heb. "ten words") have their importance singularly emphasized by their unmatched ethical majesty and by the context in which they are introduced. Both Jewish and Christian communities have recognized their unique significance and have incorporated them as an integral part of their catechetical practices. The Ten Commandments form one moral code and, apart from the particularity of the sabbath, form a clear and succinct ethical statement universally relevant to all mankind. There are no sufficient reasons to deny either their monotheistic basis or their Mosaic provenance.

The Decalogue has been conceived variously by different groups. The Roman Catholic and Lutheran churches regard the First Commandment to be Exodus 20: 4–5; and the prescriptions to worship Jahweh solely and to eschew images are considered one. The number ten (Ex. 34:28; Deut. 4:13; 10:4) is then achieved by subdividing verse 17, so that the Ninth Commandment concerns coveting a neighbor's house while the Tenth has reference to his wife, manservant, and so on. The traditional Jewish division of the Commandments considers the First to be Exodus 20:2: "I am Jahweh your God, who brought you out of the land of Egypt, out of the house of bondage." The Second Commandment includes verses 3–6, prohibition of any other god, or of the making of any image or its adoration, while the Third Commandment is contained in verse 7.

The Church of England, the Greek, and Reformed churches have followed the practice of viewing the Commandments as follows: the First, monotheism (v. 3); the Second, idolatry forbidden (vv. 4–6, notice the motivation in vv. 5*b*–6); the Third, blasphemy forbidden (v. 7); the Fourth, the observance of the sabbath (vv. 8–11); the Fifth, parental honor (v. 12); the Sixth, murder prohibited (v. 13, *murder* is the correct rendering); the Seventh, adultery prohibited (v. 7), the Eighth, theft prohibited (v. 15); the Ninth, perjury forbidden (v. 16), and the Tenth, covetousness forbidden, both act and intent (v. 17).

To the individual, as to the Pharisaic mind of old, who in his self-idolatrous vanity imagines himself capable of keeping the Commandments on a purely legalistic basis, the expansive demand of the code soon becomes his condemnation. Responsible to keep *all* the law (*totum;* cp. James 2:10), to keep it with *all* his being (*toti;* cp. Ex. 6:4 ff.; Mark 12:29 f.), and to keep it *always* (*semper*), he is fractured by its inexorable exactions. The Commandments are not to be understood negatively only, but positively, as applicable to overt act, to be sure, but more inwardly directed to its intent.

There is a continuity between those who in the old dispensation and those in the new dispensation who have believed God with self-committing faith and expressed this union of faith in consonant patterns of obedience. Whether Abraham, father of the faithful, Peter, Isaiah the prophet, John the seer, Moses the servant of God, or Paul the apostle, each discovered the enabling grace of God for nobility of life by his firm attachment of faith. And a fitting epitome of their common experience may be taken from the words once used to describe the priest.

> My covenant with him [i.e., Levi] was a covenant of life and peace, and I gave them to him that he might fear; and he feared me, he stood in awe of my name. The law of truth was in his mouth, and iniquity was not found in his lips: he walked with me in peace and equity, and did turn many away

from iniquity. For the priest's lips should keep knowledge, and they should seek the law at his mouth: for he is the messenger of the LORD of hosts (Mal. 2:7 ff.).

If there were a basic continuity between the old and the new dispensation, there was also a decided cleavage. In the law of the old covenant the command regarding the sabbath prescribed rest for the total economy on pain of death (Ex. 31:12–17; compare 16:23; 35:1–3; 23:12; 34:21). A markedly different attitude toward the sabbath is encountered in the New Testament.

Never let anyone else decide what you should eat or drink, or whether you are to observe annual festivals [compare Ex. 23:14 ff.; 34:18–34] or sabbaths. These were only pale reflections of what was coming, but the reality belongs to Christ (Col. 2:16 f. *BJ*).

Circumcision was enjoined upon all Hebrews, under threat of excommunication (Gen. 17:9–14), in the old covenant, whereas in the New Testament it is dismissed summarily as a matter of indifference three times in the letters of Paul. "In Christ Jesus neither circumcision nor uncircumcision is of any avail, but faith working through love" (Gal. 5:6; see 6:15; 1 Cor. 7:19). The distinction between clean (Kosher) and unclean food (Lev. 11:1 ff.; 20:25; Deut. 14:3–9), inherited no doubt from their Semitic background, is abrogated both in the words of Jesus in the apostolic tradition. "Do you not see that whatever goes into a man from outside cannot defile him, since it enters, not his heart, but his stomach, and so passes on? [Thus he declared all foods clean.]" (Mark 7:19; cp. Luke 11:41). Deeply disturbed about the problem of eating unclean foods as he associated with Gentiles, Peter had the problem rationalized and resolved in a dream experience. In the vision he was bidden by the divine voice to rise, kill, and eat from various types of animals. Peter refused, asserting that he had never eaten anything common or unclean. To this the divine voice replied, "What God has cleansed, you must not call common" (Acts 10:15). When he awakened, he shared with the Gentile Cornelius his new conviction:

You yourselves know how unlawful it is for a Jew to associate with or to visit any one of another nation; but God has shown me that I should not call any man common or unclean (Acts 10:28).

The dietary laws of the old covenant which precluded table fellowship between Jew and Gentile are here abrogated. Christian religion repudiated the dietary laws of the old covenant and adopted an attitude of profounder insight for its practice. In 1 Timothy 4:3–5 those are not to be heard who

> enjoin abstinence from foods which God created to be received with thanksgiving by those who believe and know the truth. For everything created by God is good [compare Gen. 1:12,25], and nothing is to be rejected if it is received with thanksgiving; for then it is consecrated by the word of God and prayer.

It is not only cultic practices of the old dispensation that are substantially modified in the New Testament, but moral inadequacies are challenged and are superseded by definitive ethical principles. The law of divorce (Ex. 20:13; Deut. 15:17; 16:18), said Jesus, was a concession on the part of Moses because of the hardness of Israel's heart; but the concession would not be admitted in his religion (Matt 5:31; 19:7 f.). The *lex talionis* (Ex 21:23–25; Lev. 24:19 f.; Deut. 19:21), perhaps a necessary deterrent in early society, is not to be perpetuated in the kingdom of heaven. Mindful of other Old Testament passages of profounder spiritual insight (Lev. 19:18; Deut. 32:35; Prov. 20:22), Jesus proposed unselfishness and forgiveness instead of retaliation (Matt 5:38). The Commandments concerning adultery and murder, he affirmed, were to be deepened to include intent as well as act (Matt 5:21 ff., 27 ff.). The enemies of the Christian church saw more clearly than some of the early disciples that the religion of Jesus would "change the customs Moses delivered" (Acts 6:14; cp. 6:11). The program of Jesus was clearly and unequivocally announced in his preaching. "Think not that I have come to abolish the law and the prophets; I have come not to abolish them but to fulfil them" (Matt. 5:17). "In this process of fulfilment, all that is imperfect, provisional, temporary, or, for any reason needless to the perfect religion, falls away of its own accord, and all that is essential and permanent is conserved and embodied in Christianity." [6] Jesus came not to destroy, but to fulfill, to complete, to perfect, to emend, to give a temporary thing an eternal validity (T. H. Robinson).

C. Its Sacrament (Ex. 24)

The narrative which commences in Exodus 19 is interrupted by the Decalogue (20:1–17); it resumes in Exodus 20:18–21, where again its flow is broken by the covenant code (20:22–26 supplementary laws; and the code itself (chs. 21:1 to 23:33), then the narrative continues in Exodus 24.

After the terms of the covenant agreement had been recited and confirmed by the shaking of hands (cp. Isa. 2:6*c*; Job 17:3; Prov. 22:26), the parties normally passed between severed sacrifice by which act they became sacramentally united in the covenantal relationship. This is the significance of the liturgy described in Exodus 24.

The first part of this narrative is not without its difficulties. If, however, the substantive repetitions (v.3 = v.7; v.6= v.8) are recognized, and if verse 4 has its opening phrase rendered as: "now Moses having written the words of Jahweh, rose up . . . .", the order of events becomes tolerably clear. The narrative itself commences with the divine injunction to Moses to assemble the people and its leader in the plain some distance removed from the mountain. Moses alone is to approach the divine presence as the celebrant of the covenantal sacrament. An altar and twelve standing pillars, symbolic of the number of the tribes of Israel, are erected at the foot of the mountain. Burnt offerings and peace offerings are then sacrificed. While the burnt offering except its blood is totally devoted to the altar fire, the peace offering has a portion placed on the altar, the remainder used to provide a sacred feast for the worshipers. Moses next read the scroll containing the words of the covenant to which the people responded affirmatively.

After the verbal part of the liturgy between the covenanting parties was recited, the sacrament of the sacrifice was performed with half of the sacrificial blood being dashed against the altar, signifying the covenanting God, and half of it was sprinkled upon the pillars and the people. As this ceremony was in process, Moses recited the liturgical words: "Behold the blood of the covenant which Jahweh has made with you in accordance with all these words" (v. 8). The epistle to the Hebrews restates this liturgy as follows:

> even the first covenant was not ratified without blood, for when every commandment of the law had been declared by Moses to all the people, he took the blood of calves and goats, with water and scarlet wool and hyssop, and sprinkled both the book itself and all the people, saying, "This is the blood of the covenant which God commanded you" (9:19–20).

The important point here affirmed is that the solemnization or ratification was through the sacramental word and act.

Once the covenant was consummated, Moses, Aaron and his two sons, Nadab and Abihu, together with the elders of Israel approached nearer (cp. v. 2) and, as representative of the nation, partook of the covenantal meal. It may be imagined that the dark tempestuous storm clouds had been dissipating somewhat, and now as they were near the Presence, partaking of the holy meal and conscious of sharing a covenant with Jahweh, a break in the clouds above the mountain suddenly gave way to the deep azure blue of the cloudless sky beyond. It was a beatific vision, so symbolic of the moment, not unlike the prophet Isaiah's: "they saw the God of Israel and there was under his feet as it were a pavement of sapphire stone, like the very heaven for clearness" (v. 10).

With this one may compare the descriptions of the theophanic Presence elaborated in Ezekiel (1:4–28; 8:1–4). The motifs of the thunderstorm (1:4, 28) and the ethereal glory of the heavens (1:22), the oblique language ("the likeness of . . . ," "as it were . . . ," etc.) and the reticence to describe God except in the vaguest terms and similes (1:26 f.; 8:2) parallel the vision of God in Exodus 24. The only particular of the vision is Exodus 24:10: "there was under his feet as it were . . . ." words somewhat parallel to Ezekiel 1:27 and 8:2. One may add to this discussion the interpretation of the bow in the sky in Genesis 9:8–17. Hebrew has no word for "rainbow"; the word used in that chapter denotes the bow of an archer. During the raging of the flood Jahweh appeared like a warrior armed with bow and arrow; but after the flood, like a warrior returning home removes his bow from his shoulder and hangs it up upon the wall, Jahweh placed his bow in the sky to denote his good will toward man and to indicate the guarantee of seasonal return. The ancients saw in that glorious prismatic bow a divine communication of promise and assurance exalted in the sky after the dark storm clouds of the flood.

In Exodus 24:10 f. the leaders of Israel are described as having seen the God of Israel. However, in Exodus 33:20 Moses is warned that he cannot see God's face, for no man can see him and live. The seeming incongruity is the Hebraic way of affirming both the transcendence of God and his immanence. The same type of problem may be found in the role that the Temple played in Israel. Solomon had built it as a house of habitation for Jahweh, a place for him to dwell in forever (1 Kings 8:13); yet in the same chapter his words present the paradox: "But will God indeed dwell on the earth? Behold, heaven and the highest heaven cannot contain thee; how much less this house which I have built" (v. 27). It is the affirmation of faith that the transcendent has a sacramental immanence, that God who is everywhere is not nowhere, but rather is somewhere. The paradox of faith is that the leaders of Israel saw the invisible God (cp. Heb. 11:27).

The second block of materials in Exodus 24 relates the ascent of Moses into the mount to receive the tables of stone (v. 12 ff.). Leaving Aaron and Hur in charge of the camp, Moses proceeded with his servant Joshua to ascend the mountain. Clouds and fire marked the summit of the mount in the view of the people, a description which may have its basis in the fire and smoke insignia of Jahweh's presence interpreted as the pillar of fire and of cloud and accompanying Moses in his ascent. After six days Jahweh called to Moses out of the midst of the cloud; Moses entered the cloud and was there for forty days.

Theological Reflections. What the wedding ceremony is to marriage, what the impression of the seal is to a document, the sacrament in Exodus 24 was to the Sinaitic covenant. It was its validation, the climax and seal of the agreement, the union of parties to an agreement in a liturgy of solemnization.

The religion of Jesus Christ is entered into as a covenantal agreement. Against the expressiveness of the Passover Jesus introduced the new covenant. In a sense it was an old covenant because it embodied within itself all the eternal and universal promises of the patriarchal covenants, all the eternal verities of the Sinaitic covenant. It had affinities to the thought pattern of John as he wrote of the continuity and discontinuity of the commandment.

> Dear friends, I give you no new command. It is the old command which you always had before you; the old command is the message which you heard at the beginning [i.e. the commandment of love]. And yet again it is a new command that I am giving you—new in the sense that darkness is passing and the real light already shines. Christ has made this true and it is true in your own experience (1 John 2:7–8 f., NEB).

It is a profoundly moving thought that the church of God shares the blessings promised in the former covenants, that we belong to the people of God of yesteryears (Hos 2:23; 1 Pet. 2:10; cp. John 4,38*b*), that we are the spiritual children of Abraham (Rom. 4:11,16 f.; Gal. 3:7; cp. Matt 3:9) and heirs according to promise (Gal. 3:29), and that in the fullest sense we sit at table with Abraham, Isaac, and Jacob in the kingdom of heaven (Matt. 8:11; Eph. 3:15; Heb. 11:40). It is the communion of saints in covenant. And yet despite this glorious continuity with the old, there is something definitive, unique, transcendent, eternal in the new covenant, vistas of meaning which many prophets and righteous men longed to see and to hear (Matt. 3:17), things into which angels longed to look (1 Pet. 1:12).

If the old covenant had splendor, it was eclipsed by the greater glory of the new covenant! Where can one find in the old covenant an incarnate God, hear comparable words, or witness such mighty works? Where can one discover in the old covenant anything approaching the meaning of the redemptive crucifixion of Jesus, or his triumph over death for the enrichment of his mortal followers, and his transcendental ascent, bringing humanity to heaven itself? These are the better promises (Heb. 8:6); this is discontinuity with the old; this is why the covenant of Christ must be called "the new covenant."

In the upper room, at the Passover liturgy, the Lord took the unleavened bread, blessed it, broke it, distributed it, and interpreted it with these words: "Take, eat; this is my body" (Matt. 26:26). With the chalice of wine in his hand, he blessed it, drank of it, passed it to his disciples, and said, "This cup is the new covenant in my blood" (1 Cor. 11:25).

The moment of the new covenant envisioned by Jeremiah had arrived.

> Behold, the days are coming, says Jahweh, when I will make a new covenant with the house of Israel and the house of Judah, not like the covenant which I made with their fathers when I took them by the hand to bring them out of the land of Egypt, my covenant which they broke, though I was their husband, says Jahweh. But this is the covenant which I will make with the house of Israel after those days, says Jahweh; I will put my law within them, and I will write it upon their hearts; and I will be their God, and they shall be my people. And no longer shall each man teach his neighbor and each his brother, saying, 'Know Jahweh,' for they shall all know me, from the least of them to the greatest, says Jahweh; for I will forgive their iniquity, and I will remember their sin no more (Jer. 31:31–34).

Unlike the old dispensation, where the law was carved in letters on stone, the new covenant provided that the law be inscribed upon the human heart. There would be a profounder unity between God and his people: what a God ought to be to his people, that he would be; what a people ought to be in regard to their God, that they would be enabled to become. The knowledge of God, that insight into the Divine where to know was to be, would be the possession of the members of the new covenant (cp. Jer. 22:16; Hos. 6:6 contrasted with Hos. 4:1,6; Jer. 9:3; John 17:3; 1 John 4:7 f.). The better sacrifice upon which the new covenant was founded (Heb. 9:23), effectively atoned for human sin.

> The range of Levitical atonements was very narrow. They were confined to bodily impurity, ceremonial offences, sins of ignorance, and certain specified offences (Lev. vi. 1,7; xxix.20). They did not deal with moral offences as such; they had no relief for 'high-handed sins' [7] (Cp. Num. 15: 30 f.).

This inadequacy contrasts sharply with the munificent forgiveness available in the new covenant.

> How much more [than the repetitious, inadequate Levitical sacrifice] shall the blood of Christ, who through the eternal Spirit offered himself without blemish to God, purify your conscience from dead works to serve

the living God (Heb. 9:14)

We have been sanctified through the offering of the body of Jesus Christ once for all (Heb. 10:10).

As Moses sprinkled the altar, the people, and the scroll to effect the sacramental unity (Ex. 24:6–8; Heb. 9:18 ff.) the sacrifice of Christ unites us with him and his gospel in indissoluble bonds.[8] Each time the new covenant is reaffirmed in the Lord's Supper, one feels its verities anew in the bond of unity (1 Cor. 10:16 f.). And if Moses and the elders ate and drank in the sacramental meal and saw God, how much more the Christian at the Lord's board! If they saw the azure sky in its clarity after its ominous storm and interpreted the vision as the symbol of Jahweh's goodness, how much more do we see the glory of God in the face of Jesus Christ (2 Cor. 4:6). The church does not approach the foreboding and forbidding mount with its blazing fire, darkness, gloom, and trumpet; it draws near to Jesus the mediator of a new and better covenant (Heb. 12:18–24). In many ways the writer of the epistle to the Hebrews is more deeply sensitized to the splendor of the Levitical worship than any other writer in the New Testament, and yet despite this appreciation he recognized its deficiencies and its inadequacies. For him, and for the Christian church, the new covenant was better than the old (Heb. 7:22; 8:6). It was founded on better promises (Heb. 8:6), possessed of a better sacrifice (Heb. 9:23), a better hope (Heb. 7:19), a better country to anticipate than Canaan (Heb. 11:16), and a better resurrection (Heb. 11:35), not dimly suggested, but explicitly exhibited in the resurrection of Jesus.

The entire purpose of the tabernacle may be summed up in the verse: "Let them make me a sanctuary, that I may dwell in their midst" (Ex. 25:8; 29:45 f.). It was, as Paul pointed out, a unique and blessed experience of Israel. But the greater tabernacling (and the diction is the very same) was not in a cloud but in a human personality, when the Word who was God assumed flesh, and tabernacled among us, and exhibited that glory commensurate with his identity (John 1:14,18). In the words of T. W. Manson:

[In the Old Testament] we get glimpses of the character of God. But . . . to know God fully one must live with Him. The claim of the New Testament is that the full revelation did come in that way. "The Word became flesh and dwelt among us." To put it in another way, the fullest revelation could not be made in terms of isolated acts or messages [compare Heb. 1:1]; it could only be made in terms of personality and life: and the personality and life were the personality and life of Jesus of Nazareth. If that claim is just it means that the Biblical revelation is final, in the sense that all is revealed there that men can possibly take in. It is a revelation in terms of the highest category we can know—that of personality.[9]

NOTES

[1] *Moses. The Revelation and the Covenant.* New York: Harper & Brothers, 1958, p. 110.

[2] *The Life of Christ in Recent Research.* New York: Oxford University Press, 1907, p. 19.

[3] *Zeitschrift für kirchlichen Wissenschaft und kirchlichen Leben,* 1882, p. 298, quoted by S. R. Driver, *Exodus.* Cambridge at the University Press, 1929, p. 177.

[4] *Moses. The Revelation and the Covenant.* New York: Harper & Brothers, 1946, p. 110.

[5] The identifications turn on the prepositions. The Gentiles are *outside the law* (Gk. *anomos* = *a* is alpha privative or negative + *nomos,* law); the legalistic Jews are *under the law* (Gk. *hupo nomon);* but the Christian is *enlawed* of Christ (Gk. *ennomos* =*en,* in + *nomos,* law), that is, the law is *in,* at the very essence of his being and at the fountain of his motivation.

[6] George B. Stevens, *The Theology of the New Testament.* New York: Charles Scribner's Sons, 1899, 19. Chapter II, "The Gospel and the Law" is indispensable reading for all who seek enlightenment on this subject.

[7] B. F. Westcott, *The Epistle to the Hebrews.* London: Macmillan & Co., 1889, 288f.

[8] There are no parallels in the Old Testament comparable to such divine-human fellowship as is promised in John 6:56 f.; and 17:11,22 ff.

[9] T. W. Manson, ed. *A Companion to the Bible.* Edinburgh: T. & T. Clark, 1939, p. 9.

V

Israel's Worship

(25—40)

A. The Tabernacle (Ex. 25—27; 35—38; 40)

The extended description of the portable sanctuary and the investiture of the Aaronic priesthood constantly reappear in the ongoing history of Israel. They become important for religious understanding since so many later theological ideas are cast in a priestly form. Prophets and psalmists, historians and apocalyptists develop the symbols and interpret religion from the suggestive ideas regarding the sanctuary and the priesthood. The New Testament is deeply indebted to this block of materials for some of its basic ideas. The very purpose of the sanctuary was that Jahweh might dwell in the midst of Israel (25:8).

In Exodus 25—27,30 Moses is instructed how to build the tabernacle; in chapters 35—38 the accomplishment of the several tasks is noticed; accordingly, there is considerable duplication though each account has some important details not included in its counterpart.

The historicity of the tabernacle cannot be seriously questioned. Dr. W. F. Albright states: "After the demonstration by R. Hartmann and especially by H. Lammens of nomadic Arab parallels to the portable Tabernacle and Ark of the Covenant, some of them going far back into pre-Islamic times, it is captious to refuse them Mosaic date, since they are completely foreign to sedentary Canaanite practice and since they are known to have persisted for some time after the Conquest of Palestine." [1]

The account of the construction of the tabernacle opens with an inventory of materials contributed by the people (25:1–9; 35:4–29). The sole piece of furniture in the holy of holies was the ark of the covenant (25:10–22; 37:1–9). It consisted of two parts: the box of acacia wood overlaid with gold leaf and the cover or lid of purest gold with cherubic figures at each end facing one another with their wings spread out. The ark was considered to be the symbolic conveyance of Jahweh (Num. 10:35 f.) who deigned to be enthroned between the cherubim (Ps. 80:1; Num. 7:89). The covering of the chest became the focus of all else in the tabernacle; it was there the heavenly met the earthly in the mediation of the revelation and in the forgiving divine grace. The latter is well conveyed when the covering became the "mercy seat" in the Greek translation of the Old Testament (cp. the ritual of the Day of Covering, "Yom Kippur," in Lev. 16:14–16).

Attention moves to the furniture in the holy place, outside the inner veil. The table of showbread is described (Ex. 25:23–30; 37:10–16) with its tableware. Twelve biscuits of bread and drafts of wine were placed upon the table each week and were representatively eaten by the priests in a ritual involving incense as they shared the divine board. The golden candlestick (25:31–40; 37:17–24), better, candelabrum, with its central shaft was flanked on either side with three branches. On the apex of each branch there were removable lamps which burned olive oil with a wick of tow and were to be attended morning and evening (Ex. 27:20 f.). The almond flower and fruit were the motif for the candelabrum.

The third article in the holy place was the altar of incense (30:1–10; 37:25–28) whose location was immediately before the interior veil. Its purpose was to provide a fitting aroma for the sanctuary each morning and evening. Firestones, no doubt heated at the brazen altar, were conveyed to the altar of incense and placed in censers on the altar top. Incense was then sprinkled upon the hot stones and gave forth its fragrance. The preparation of the incense is described in Exodus 30:34–38 (cp. 37:29); its use was restricted to the divine service alone (v. 38).

The framework of the tabernacle consisted of a series of boards each of which was fifteen feet high and twenty-seven inches wide, made of acacia wood overlaid with gold (Ex. 26:15–30; 36:20–34). There were twenty boards on each side connected with eight others at the rear. This U-shape series of upright boards was held together by exterior ring attachments and transversal poles. Each board had two tenons which fitted into mortars of brick weights so that the board itself did not rest upon the ground and was secured. The interior face of each board had a clasp from which the loops of blue in the draperies hung.

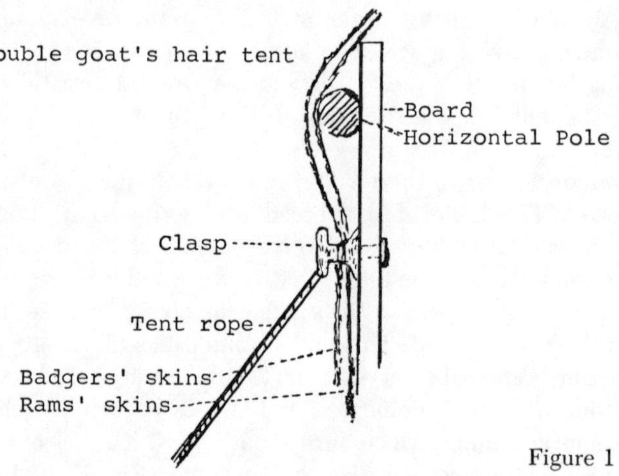

Figure 1

The interior drapes were made with a linen warp with a blue, purple, and scarlet woof (26:1–6; 38:8–13). Cherubic figures were embroidered upon them with gold thread while loops of blue were attached to their upper borders. The loops of blue were hung on the interior knobs located some seven feet from the ground apparently. The two drapes were superimposed one on the other, a doubling of materials as obtains elsewhere in the tabernacle. The consummate artistry of Near Eastern weavers is proverbial. It may be well assumed that it was not absent here.

In the tabernacle there were two veils: an outer and an inner veil. The inner veil (Ex. 26:31–36) had the same manufacture as the interior drapes. It was supported by five upright posts, secured in weights, and hung by its loops of blue. It separated the holy of holies from the holy place (see Figure 2). Beyond the inner veil only the high priest could go, and that once a year, on the Day of Atonement (Lev. 16).

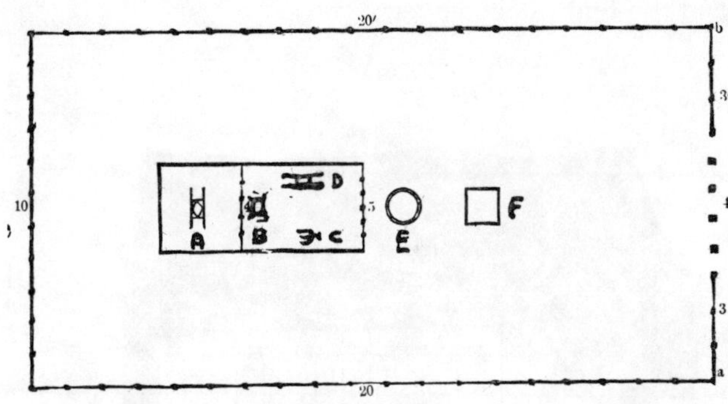

A Ark of Covenant in Holy of Holies
B Altar of Incense
C Candlestick
D Table of Showbread
E Laver
F Brazen Altar

Figure 2

The outer veil (26:36–37; 36:37 f.) resembled the inner veil except that it lacked the embroidery of the cherubic figures. Essentially it was the entrance to the sanctuary. It was also provided with loops of blue and hung by rods joining the five posts which spanned the width of the holy place.

The roof and side curtains (25:7–14; 36:14–19) formed the sheltering cover over the tabernacle (25:7; 36:14). The roof curtains were woven of black goat's hair and were joined in the manner illustrated in Figure 1. The two curtains were provided with loops of blue on both outer edges which were attached as Figure 1 depicts. The roof and the side curtains were doubled to insure protection against moisture. The eleventh curtain of the roof structure was folded to cover the space between the ridge and eaves of the rear of the tabernacle. The side curtains were made of tanned rams' skins and goatskins and protected the three sides of the tabernacle's framework of boards (see Figure 3). The description makes a clear demarcation between the tabernacle (framework of boards and two veils) and the tent pitched over it.

Figure 3

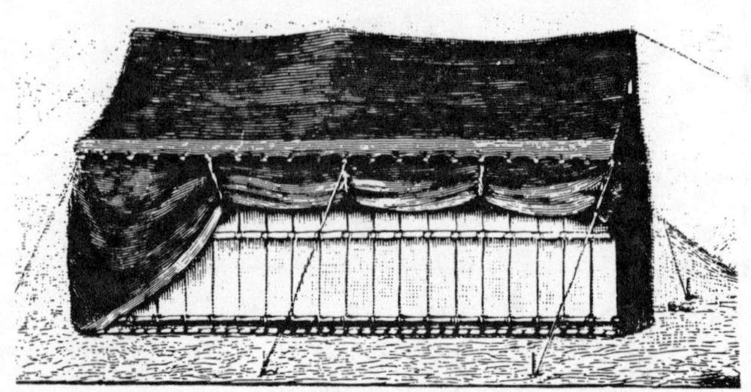

The tabernacle was considered the symbolic house where Jahweh dwelt (Ex. 25:8). It was patterned in accordance with the finest of nomadic dwellings. It was never intended to be an auditorium. In accordance with its purpose its dimensions were quite small. It was forty-five feet long with fifteen feet as its width and height. With true oriental reserve Jahweh had his point of contact with his appointed priestly ministers who in turn mediated his will to the people.

The outer court of the sanctuary measured one hundred fifty by seventy-five feet and was marked off by a white linen fence some seven and a half feet high, supported on sixty posts secured in bronze sockets. Four of these posts supported the entrance gate on the east which had curtains woven of blue, purple, and scarlet some thirty feet in width.

The brazen altar (27:1–8; 38:1–7) was located not far from the entrance gate on a line between that gate and the sanctuary itself (see Figure 3). It was seven and a half feet square and four and a half feet high, provided with all the utensils necessary for sacrifice.

Between the brazen altar and the sanctuary was a large receptacle of water known as the laver (30:17–21; 38:8), presumably round in shape, that served to wash the hands and feet of the ministering priests.

The importance of the tabernacle was admirably summed up by Bishop Westcott:

> It had lessons to teach. It witnessed to the needs of men; and yet the whole ritual it embodied could not reach beyond the outward and visible (ix. 10,12). Thus we see in the Epistle to the Hebrews that the Levitical system discharged a two-fold office. It had an educational value, as enforcing the great thoughts of Judaism, and it had also an immediate value, as dealing under the conditions of the Mosaic Covenant with the sins and weaknesses of the people of God.[2]

Theological Reflections. Considerable insight into the religious ideas of the Old Testament may be gained by an exploration of their earliest antecedents. Centuries before the Hebrews emerged into history, the ancient Near East conceived of their gods and his service as analogous to their king and his reign. The king was lord and owner of the land, dwelt in the palace, was regally attired, maintained a lavish table, held court and council while seated upon his throne, possessed a diplomatic corps, an army, house servants, musicians, privy council, each with his appropriate livery, and prescribed the law and the calendar for the land. The deity had attributed to him these kingly prerogatives on a grander scale. The god had his palace or temple. The same Hebrew term *hekhal* means both and is a loanword from the Sumerians, borrowed by the Canaanites before 2500 B.C., and assimilated into the proto-Hebraic vocabulary. The Egyptian term *pharaoh* in its earlier use meant "the great house." The god possessed the land (Gen. 14:19,22; Ex. 19:5); its population was his servants (Ex. 10:6; 32:13,42). His clothing befitted his station, at times its dyes were exclusively royal (see Isa. 6; Ex. 20:33,38). His council is pictured as heavenly hosts (cp. Job 1:6; 2:1; 1 Kings 22:19 ff.) as it deliberates the divine counsel (Jer. 23:18,22; Amos 3:7). The diplomatic corps is his means of communication to the people; they are his spokesmen, dispatched with his message (the prophets; see Jer. 25:4; 26:5; 29:19). His high officials carried out the divine instructions and supervised his servants (cp. 1 Kings 4:1–6). The priesthood provided the sustenance for the divine table. At times this early background is apparent in some of the language of the Old Testament though the thought has become entirely symbolic. The sacrifices are called "the food of God" or "the bread of God" (Lev. 3:16; 21:6,8,17,21 f.; 22:25), "my food" (Ezek. 44:7; Num. 28:2; cp. 28:24) while the altar is termed "the table of Jahweh" (Mal. 1:7,12). The tabernacle with its costly furnishings represents the finest of palatial splendor in a seminomadic culture and reflects in a symbolic way their dedication to their God.

It is somewhat of a surprise to discover that the outer court was only 150 by 75 feet marked by a linen barricade some 7½ feet high. The entrance of the court was 37½ feet wide and faced the east. The house of Jahweh was not public domain; it was off limits to practically everyone other than those who approached its gate in a cultic matter. The sacrifices were brought to the gate of the tabernacle and dedicated there. It suggests little democracy in the religious experience; it was the priest who provided the liaison between Jahweh and the people. Religion of the common man was mediated and at a distance.

The brazen altar with its horns of bronze was the place where the various sacrifices were offered. The fat and blood were burned on the altar while the other portions of the sacrifice were dealt with according to the type offered. The covenant at Sinai was basically one involving an ethical relationship between God and Israel; the sacrifice of animals was decidedly secondary. It may be admitted that it took a long period before this was clearly perceived.

> In the day that I brought them out of the land of Egypt, I did not speak to your fathers or command them concerning burnt offerings and sacrifices; but this command I gave them, Obey my voice and I will be your God and you shall be my people; and walk in all the way that I command you that it may be well with you (Jer. 7:22 f.).

Isaiah, Jeremiah, Micah, Amos, and Hosea inveighed against the perversion of cultic sacrifice as a cover-up for gross sinfulness. Some of the psalmists wonder how an animal with horns and hoofs can effect the deep spiritual strivings in their souls and maintain that the only true sacrifice that avails before Jahweh is a broken and contrite heart (Ps. 40:6–8; 50:12–16; 51:16–17). Christianity affirms that the death of Christ fulfilled the sacrificial ideal once and for all, that sacrifices need never again be repeated year by year, and that uniquely our Lord offered himself to purge us from dead works to serve the true and the living God and that in the relevant terms of his incarnation (Heb. 2:14–18; 9:11–14; 10:1–12). The incomparable glory of the sacrifice of Jesus has provided his followers with an altar whereof those who serve the tent (that is, the sacrificial system of Israel) have no right to eat (that is, partake of his sacrifice in salvation and sustenance) (Heb. 13:10–11).

The laver provided a facility for Aaron and the priests to wash their hands and their feet before entering the tent of meeting (Ex. 40:30–32) or ministering at the altar (Ex. 30:18–21; cp. Heb. 9:10; 10:22).

The tabernacle proper was quite diminutive, but formed the focal point where the priests might function as the representatives of the people in the service of God. The table of showbread with its cups of wine represented by its number of loaves the twelve tribes of Israel. The priests ate the sacramental meal of bread and wine while incense was rising from the table thus signifying that the mighty Lord Jahweh deigned to eat with his people in close table fellowship and provided for them the sustenance needful for their days.

The candelabrum with its seven lamps furnished the illumination within the tabernacle. The number of its stems was seven, their motif was the almond; the oil was unique and excluded from common use; the lamps burned continuously. All this is quite symbolic with seven as a holy number (for example, seven days of creation, sabbath, the word *oath* comes from the number itself); the almond suggests the ever-vigilant God (Jer. 1:11 f.) whose unique light perennially dispels the darkness. In the Revelation the high priestly ministry of Jesus toward his churches is indicated as the seer sees one like the Son of man in priestly garments amid the seven golden lampstands. (Rev. 1:12 ff.)

The altar of incense stood before the inner veil. The service of the priests was accompanied by the burning of incense upon this altar. The fragrance conveyed the sense of acceptance as evening and morning sacrifice and the prayers of the people were simultaneously offered with the ascending fragrance (Ex. 30:7 f.; Ps. 141:2; Luke 1:8 ff.)

The veil that separated the two portions of the tabernacle, later known in the Solomonic and subsequent temples in Jerusalem as the veil in the Temple (Matt 27:51), was entered once a year, on the Day of Atonement. The epistle to the Hebrews points out that in the old dispensation the way into the holiest of all was barred by the veil (Heb. 9:3,7 f.), but in the death of Christ the veil in the Temple was rent from the top to the bottom, opening once and for all the way into the holiest of all to the entire household of faith (Heb. 10:19–23; 6:19).[3]

In the inner room, known later as the holy of holies or the oracle, was the ark of the covenant. Within the chest were the two tablets Moses received, a pot of manna, and subsequently, the rod of Aaron that had budded. If the Decalogue is the expression of righteousness and morality, perhaps we are not without justification to see a reference to the ark in an expression of one of the psalmists. "Righteousness and justice are the foundation of his throne" (Ps. 97:2*b*). The ark with its guardian cherubim was considered the throne of Jahweh.

> He sits enthroned upon the cherubim;
> let the earth quake! (Ps. 99:1*b*).

> Thou who art enthroned upon the cherubim,
> shine faith before Ephraim and Benjamin and Manasseh (Ps. 80:1*b*–2*a*; cp. 1 Sam. 4:4; 2 Sam. 6:2).

The lid (Heb., *kipporeth*, "covering") assumed the focus of attention on the annual Day of Atonement (Yom Kippur), for it was there that the high priest sprinkled with his finger seven times the blood of his own atoning sacrifice and that of the people's sacrifice (Lev. 16:14–15). When the Hebrew Scriptures were translated into Greek, the word for lid was rendered *hilasterion*, "mercy seat." This term, which is elsewhere translated as "propitiation," was used by Paul in his definite presentation of the nature of Christ's death.

> . . . being justified freely by his grace, through the redemption that is in

> Christ Jesus, whom God hath set forth to be a *propitiation* in his blood, to be received by faith (Rom. 3:24 f.).

Propitiation may be defined as that aspect of the sacrifice of Christ that satisfies the divine demands; the sin is expiated, and the sinner reconciled. John employs the same term and for the same purpose (1 John 2:2; 4:10). At the very throne of Jahweh the blood of Christ's propitiatory sacrifice has effected forgiveness for us. We are, therefore, bidden to draw near to God with a true heart

> . . . since we have confidence to enter the sanctuary by the blood of Jesus by the new and living way which he opened for us through the curtain, that is, through his flesh (Heb. 10:19–20; cp. 4:16; Matt. 27:51).

B. The Aaronic Priesthood (Ex. 28—29,39)

The garments of the high priest (28:1–43; 39:1–31) were designed to convey symbolically the significance of the priesthood generally and reflect the glory of the God in whose service they were worn. In the instruction provided for their creation it is specifically stated that they were to be "for beauty and for glory" (28:1–4; 39:1).

The robe of the ephod was a full-length robe similar to a sleeveless cassock and drawn over the head, with a woven border around the neck. At the base of its skirt, models of pomegranates made of blue, purple, and scarlet yarn alternated with little golden bells which sounded when the high priest moved (28:31–35; 39:22–26).

The ephod (28:5–15; 39:2–7) which was worn over the robe of blue was a vest or waistcoat, supported at the shoulders by two large onyx stones on which were inscribed the names of the tribes of Israel, and girded about the waist at its lower border. The garment was woven of blue, purple, and scarlet materials.

The breastplate of judgment (28:13–30; 39:8–21) was the most significant part of the high priest's raiment. Essentially it was a pouch some nine inches square, woven from blue, purple, and scarlet materials and embroidered with gold thread. Its exterior side bore gold settings enclosing four rows of precious stones with three stones to each row. Each stone had inscribed in it one of the names of the tribes of Israel. The breastplate was secured to the ephod by two golden chains and a cord of blue. Connected with the breastplate were the Urim and Thummim, presumably the positive and negative signs which are used in the obtaining of oracles (Lev. 8:8; cp. 1 Sam. 14:41 f., where they are connected with the casting of lots).

The high priest wore a linen tunic or coat of fine linen (28:39; 39:27) as his outer garment which was girded about with a sash. On his head he wore a turban of white linen with a gold plate bearing the inscription, "Holiness to Jahweh," attached to the front of the turban by a cord of blue (28:36–38; Lev. 8:9; 39:30 f.).

The ordinary priests were provided with tunics (coats) and sashes to be worn over linen breeches as well as turbans for their heads (28:40–43; 39:27–29). These, too, were garments for glory and for beauty.

The Investiture of the Priesthood (Ex. 29; Lev. 8). The account commences with the enumeration of the sacramental material: a bullock for a sin offering, two rams one for a burnt offering, the other, called "the ram of Aaron's ordination" (vv. 22,26), for a peace offering, together with unleavened bread, cakes, and wafers. The ceremonial liturgy began with the gathering of the congregation at the Tent of Meeting to witness the consecration. Aaron and his sons washed themselves and were invested in their holy garments (vv. 4–9; Lev. 8:6–9). The bullock was then offered for a sin offering (vv. 4–10). The priests imposed their hands upon the animal's head (a ritual known as the *semicah*), identifying themselves with the sacrifice. Its fat and kidneys were burned on the altar while its blood was dashed at the base of the altar; the rest of the animal was burned outside the camp in accordance with the sin offering ritual.

One of the rams was offered as a burnt offering with its quartered parts being consumed on the altar. Again, the imposition of hands and the dashing of blood against the altar took place (vv. 15–18).

The other ram was then offered as a peace offering. After the imposition of hands upon its head, it was slain with part of its blood dashed against the altar while the other part was used to touch the right ears, the right thumbs, and the right feet of Aaron and his sons. At this juncture the priests and their garments were sprinkled with the sacrificial blood and the anointing oil (vv. 19–21; Lev. 8:12,30), whose preparation and purpose are described in Exodus 30:22; 37:29; cp. Lev. 8:10–11, where the sanctuary is sanctified with the sacred oil). The application of the blood to the altar, representing Jahweh, and to the person and garments of the priests accompanied by the sprinkling of the anointing oil consecrated (hallowed) the priesthood (v. 21).

The congregation was witness of this ritual in which the priests had become holy and were thus enabled to minister in the service of Jahweh without danger. Now the people were to witness another prerogative of the priest: portions of the sacrifices offered at the altar were to become their vested right. This became evident when Moses took the fat, the appendage of the liver, and the two kidneys of the ram of consecration and with one loaf of bread, one cake, and one wafer and waved them before Jahweh, that is, moved them back and forth to acknowledge symbolically their divine provenance and their present dedication, after which they were burned on the altar. But the breast of the ram, after having been waved as a wave offering before Jahweh, became the portion of Moses as with similar ceremony the thigh became the property of Aaron and his sons. Thus was initiated the practice which obtained in Israel for the support of the priesthood (v. 28; cp. 1 Sam. 2:12–17).

The ceremony concluded with a sacred meal at the gate of the sanctuary in which the priests alone ate their portion of the ram of consecration with the unleavened bread that remained.

The consecration ritual lasted seven days. Each day witnessed a sin offering being sacrificed on the brazen altar in order to establish its sanctity; moreover, the morning and evening offering of a year old lamb with flour, oil, and wine was prescribed as the continual burnt offering to be observed perpetually.

The purpose of the consecration of the sanctuary was to provide a suitable place "where I [Jahweh] will meet with you, to speak there to you; there I will meet with the people of Israel, and it shall be sanctified by my glory" (v. 42 f.). The consecration of Aaron and his sons was to secure their service as the priests of Jahweh (v. 44). The overarching motivation for the construction and consecration of the sanctuary and the investiture of the priests was that Jahweh might dwell among the people of Israel and be their God. Israel shall know that Jahweh is their God who brought them forth out of the land of Egypt that he might dwell among them (v. 45).

The book of Exodus concludes its description of the sanctuary with an acknowledgment of the leaders who carried out the instructions of Moses (cp. "the pattern shown thee in the mount" (Ex. 25:9,40; Num. 8:4), namely, Bezalel and Oholiab (Ex. 31:1–11; 35:30 to 36:1; 38:21–23). The work was completed (39:32–43) and the tabernacle was set up (40:1–33) with the cloud resting upon the sanctuary (40:34–38).

Theological Reflections. The priesthood in Israel had its definitive expression in the office of the high priest. Its creation was necessitated by the existing need to centralize, to regulate, and to develop the inherited patriarchal religion. There existed a danger now that there were twelve tribes to diversify and to develop religious practices peculiar to the individual tribe. Israel was basically a religious unity, and that unity needed preservation.

The Israelites in Egypt had been influenced by their cultural environment; some had defected to the service of foreign gods, Egyptian and Canaanite (Josh. 24:14 f.; Amos 5:25 ff.), and had adopted their religious practices (Ex. 32:1,4 ff.,25; Num. 24).

> The Levitical Sacrifices were based upon existing customs (Lev. xvii. 1–7). There were in some sense a concession to the spiritual immaturity of the people (Jer. vii. 22 f.); but at the same time the legislation by which they were regulated guarded them from superstitious excesses, and preserved the different true ideas to which natural sacrifice bore witness, and completed this instructive expression by fresh lessons corresponding with deeper knowledge of God and man.[4]

There is a difference between the office of the high priest and the individual serving as high priest. If one reflects on the divine-human relationship, sooner or later the need for a middle term will become apparent (Job 9:32 f.). The high priest serves as that mediator and has the investment by God and the acceptableness of man. In a word, the high priest defined and effected the optimal relationship between God and Israel. That definition was not coincident with the individual serving as high priest; the definition was symbolically framed by the structure of the office: selection by God, investment in symbolic clothing, and prescriptions for conduct.

The high priestly garments are described as "holy garments for glory and for beauty" (Ex. 28:2). As the liveried retainer reflects personally and by his attire the majesty of his master, as the magnificent clothing anthropomorphically ascribed to Jahweh (Isa. 6:1; Ps. 104:1*b*,–2*a*) and the wonderful servants who attend him (Ps. 104:4) indicate the greater glory of the Lord, the holy garments reflect the glory of the high priest's God and indicate the ministry he performs to the people. Every stage in the investiture of the high priest is regulated in accordance with the concept of holiness as Israel then perceived it. The garments were holy, Aaron was ceremonially sanctified to receive the attire; and the inscription on the gold plate attached to the mitre indicated the definitive purpose of the office, it was "holiness to Jahweh." The high priest, therefore, had the approbation of Jahweh (Heb. 5:4). His right ear, right thumb, and right toe had been touched with sacrificial bood to their purification; His garments had been sprinkled with blood and with oil (Lev. 8). The ear of the priest must be pure and responsive to hear God and the needs addressed to him (Heb. 5:2); his hand must be consecrated to his work, and his life stayed in the ways of holiness. He was the *anointed* high priest (Ex. 28:1; 29:7; 30:30) invested with exclusive ointment (Ex. 30:22–33) and admitted to a perpetual priesthood (Ex. 40:15). The successor to the office of the high priest inherited the sacerdotal attire. When Aaron died in Mount Hor, he was devested of his garments which were then immediately placed upon his son and successor Eliezer (Num. 20: 23 ff.). The priest died; long live the priest!

The high priest was not only to hear the divine word, but also to proclaim it. Associated with the breastplate of judgment were the *urim* and *thummim,* some type of oracular device not unlike the casting of lots (1 Sam. 14:41 f.). He was therefore to be a spokesman for Jahweh (compare the lingering tradition in John 11:49–52).

The work of the high priest was to maintain a holy relationship between Jahweh and his people. This was accomplished by ethical comportment and various types of ceremonies: sacrifices, ablutions, exclusions, festal observances, gifts, etc., largely contained in the books of Leviticus and Numbers. In these various rituals the clothing of the high priest indicated a quality wherewith the rite was invested. More specifically, the breastplate the high priest carried over his breast had twelve diverse, precious stones each inscribed with a name of one of the tribes of Israel. On each shoulder he wore a considerable onyx stone on which was inscribed six names of the tribes of Israel. Accordingly, wherever he went, he bore the names of his people on his heart and carried them on his shoulders. Like the stones of the breastplate, his people were precious, diverse, identified by name, yet united on one breastplate which their vicar, their representative, continually bore. The high priest and the people were one and corporately shared in his ministrations whether in the expiation of Yom Kippur, or at the altar of sacrifice, or at the time of prayer. To complement the ideal of priesthood all who had physical defect were ineligible for the office, for as the sacrifice was to be without blemish, the sacrificer must conform to the same standard (Lev. 21:16 ff.). He must have no traffic with death even though it involve his immediate family (Lev. 21:11), must not let his hair hang loose or rend his garments in grief (Lev. 21:10) which in a mild way would be tantamount to censuring a providential event. The high priest was the agent of God!

But while the Levitical priesthood was a distinct improvement over what had obtained, there were weaknesses inherent in its structure. Nowhere are these more clearly pointed out than in the Epistle to the Hebrews despite the tender sensitivity of the writer toward the cult of Israel (cp. Heb. 9:1–5).

Jesus is greater than Moses (Heb. 3:2–6), angels (Heb. 1:5–14), Abraham and Aaron (Heb. 7:4 ff.); he is not like Moses a servant in the house of God, but a Son over the house of God, and was consecrated with an oath (Heb. 7:20 f.). His priesthood is untransferable (Heb. 7:23 ff.) because he lives eternally. His ministry is not earthly or typical; it is heavenly (Heb. 9:23–28). His sacrifice had intent; it was effective within the essential sphere of reconciliation:

For if the sprinkling of defiled persons with the blood of goats and bulls and with the ashes of a heifer sanctifies for the purification of the flesh, how much more shall the blood of Christ, who through the eternal Spirit offered himself without blemish to God, purify your conscience from dead works to serve the living God (Heb. 9:13–14).

And the sacrifice that he offered is unrepeatable; it was efficacious once and for all.

Every priest stands daily at his service, offering repeatedly the same sacrifices, which can never take away sins. But when Christ had offered for all time a single sacrifice for sins, he sat down at the right hand of God (Heb. 10:11–12).

As high priest, our Lord Jesus is our advocate with the Father (1 John 2:1) and our perennial intercessor (Heb. 7:25; 9:24). When that which is perfect or complete has come, the imperfect passes away. The Levitical priests, the sacrifices, and the Temple itself have become obsolete and have passed away before the priesthood of Jesus (Heb. 8:9). All that was temporal, inadequate, typical, shadowy in the old dispensation have been superseded in Christ the ultimate reality; they have been fulfilled in him and are not longer retained in Christianity.

C. Defection and Renewal (Ex. 32—34)

The Golden Calf (Ex. 32). The narrative that has been interrupted by the description of the tabernacle and the investment of the priests (chs. 25—31) is now resumed. Moses has delayed his return from Mount Sinai for some forty days and a spirit of restlessness has seized the people. They had not distinguished themselves as imperturbable loyalists. At every crisis they murmured and were ready to capitulate to the Egyptians. With menacing tone the people bade Aaron to make gods for them which should go before them; and, as justification for this bold demand, they derogatorily reminded him that ". . . as for this Moses the man who brought us up out of the land of Egypt, we do not know what has become of him" (32:2). Under such pressure Aaron compromised and demanded gold from their rings to fabricate such an image. With a base of acacia wood—

so it would seem—Aaron had the calf overlaid with gold leaf, which was enthusiastically greeted with the defiant cry: "*These* are your gods, O Israel, who brought you up out of the land of Egypt!" To compound the atrocity Aaron erected an altar before it and proclaimed that on the morrow there would be a feast to Jahweh. The next day, "early in the morning, the people rose up, sacrificed burnt offering and peace offerings," (which latter provided food for the feast), after which "the people sat down to eat and drink, and rose up to play" (cp. vv. 19,25).

In Exodus 32:7–14 the narrative shifts to Mount Sinai to record the reaction of Jahweh. In a bold anthropomorphic scene, comparable to that where Abraham pleads before Jahweh (Gen. 18:22–33), the disappointment of Jahweh is poignantly portrayed, yet ultimately gives way to forbearance and fidelity (cp. similar tensions resolved into compassion in Hos. 11:8 f.). The greatness of Moses in his self-effacing dedication to the potential of his people stands in sharp contrast to his brother's unworthy temporizing.

As Moses and his servant Joshua approached the camp, they heard the boisterous sounds of revelry. The people had broken loose from the moral greatness of Jahwism and were grossly indulging their base passions in wine, women, and song—a shameful performance for their detractors to witness (cp. Num. 25 and Ezek. 23). Angry beyond expression, Moses cast the two tablets he had received and broke them at the foot of the mount in the sight of the people (so Deut. 9:15–17), an action that ipso facto cancelled the covenant.[5] Moses destroyed the calf in the fire and made the people drink its dust which he scattered on its surface. Aaron was confronted by his brother but again betrayed his weakness: "Not I! It was the people! Their rings I threw into the fire and lo, out popped the calf!"

The situation had gotten out of hand; now it was civil war. Segments of the people were no doubt thoroughly out of sympathy with the entire program of Moses. For them Egypt remained unquestionably the only solution. Some must have despised Moses personally because of his assumption of power and what they considered to be an arrogant autocracy. Others were disaffected by the moral constraints placed upon them and welcomed the absence of Moses as a time to give vent to their pleasure-bent drives. However, Moses rallied to his support a loyal contingent, largely from the tribe of Levi, and suppressed the rebellion at the fearful cost of three thousand lives. With the rebellion ended, the leader of Israel set all his energies to the task of repairing the breach and restoring the covenant.

In a magnificent episode the undiscourageable Moses pled before Jahweh the cause of his people and secured the reestablishment of the covenant relations (32:11–13,31–34). Nevertheless, the narrative notices that the people suffered a plague from Jahweh because of the calf (cp. Num. 25:8–9,16; 26:1) and records the dialogue between Jahweh and Moses in connection with the reluctance of Jahweh to accompany his people lest he should consume them in his anger. The plague (cp. Lev. 26:21; Ex. 36:12; Num. 16:46 ff.) illustrates ancient Israel's understanding of the role of illness within the divine economy, a view which was greatly modified in the development of religious thought particularly in the book of Job.

The dialogue between Jahweh and Moses regarding the unwillingness of Jahweh to accompany his people (33:5–17) must be understood in its anthropomorphic structure.[6] This divine-human intercommunication affirms some basic theological principles in a way and with an emphasis obtainable only in this literary form. (1) It distinguished between the essence of God and his sacramental presence. (2) Israel can be assured of the sacramental presence of Jahweh in its midst. (3) Moral aberration is of no light moment to God; he will not condone iniquity in his people. In a word, he was concerned to develop the ethical potential of Israel even though this involved discipline (Deut. 8:2–3,5). The people sensed the sobering confrontation and put off their jewelry as a sign of contrition (33:4–6).

After an historical note on the shining face of Moses, the text recounts that Moses used to pitch a tent (not to be confused with the later tabernacle) outside the camp (cp. Ex. 18:6) in order to adjudicate the complaints of the people. The tent was distinguished by the insignia of the divine (that is, the pillar of cloud/smoke) as was fitting, since the people sought Jahweh (33:7; 18:7,15 f.,19). After listening to the various cases, Moses would enter the tent to secure the divine oracle. However, his presence before Jahweh caused the skin of his face to shine so that when he returned to communicate the decision, the people were afraid. Accordingly, it became his practice to enter the divine presence with unveiled face, but when he returned to the litigants, he put a veil over his face to ally their fears. The important point in this notice is the affirmation of Israel that Moses was the mediator of the divine judgment.

When the narrative resumes, Moses is instructed to ascend the mountains alone (34:1 ff.) and to bring two tablets with him upon which Jahweh will inscribe the law. This magnificent scene is of supreme moment (33:17 to 34:9). Moses had been uncommonly bold in his discourse with Jahweh. He had secured the reinstatement of the covenant with Israel; he had been promised the Presence of Jahweh to abide in the midst of the nation. Now he arose to petition to see the glory of Jahweh! The request was impossible, for no one could see the essence of God and live (v. 20), but Jahweh would place him in the shelter of the rock and through the valley beneath would cause the external or phenomenal glory to pass in review. Passing through the defile and shielding Moses with his hand, Jahweh proclaimed his name.

> Jahweh, Jahweh, a God merciful and gracious, slow to anger, and abounding in steadfast love and faithfulness, keeping steadfast love for thousands of generations forgiving iniquity and transgression and sin, but who will by no means clear the guilty, visiting the iniquity of the fathers upon the children and upon the children's children to the third and fourth generation (Ex. 34:6 f.).

Overawed by the disclosure and mindful of Israel's plight, Moses besought earnestly the restoration of his people and their pardon as well as for the divine Presence to accompany them on their onward journey.

The narrative is broken off by a reiteration of the covenant relations between Jahweh and Israel and the prescriptions which will form the responsibilities of the people. Among these injunctions are the prohibition to make any covenant with the dwellers in Canaan, the command to destroy their cult symbols, and the command to observe what has been called the "ritual decalogue" (34:14–27) in which four of the commandments of the Decalogue are mingled with ritual ordinances.

When the narrative continues in Exodus 34:29, Moses is pictured as descending from the mount in triumph, with the glow of divine radiance on his face and the two tablets of testimony in his hand. The covenant had been restored (34:29 ff.)!

Theological Reflections. Moses had been absent in the foreboding mountain terrain for forty days. One would have imagined that the people would have been concerned for his welfare, particularly when they had received such benefits from him. At least while they were waiting, they could be expected to maintain such standards of behavior as would meet with his approval. But, alas, it was not to be.

Before the mountain where they had seen incredible events, and where they had entered into a covenant with Jahweh, they demanded a golden calf and blasphemously identified it as "these be thy gods, O Israel, which brought you up out of the land of Egypt" (Ex. 32:8). How soon we forget!

It should be of concern to all of us that in the discourse Jahweh held with Moses, there was a deep disappointment felt by Jahweh with his people, disappointment that they did not see their own true future and chose rather the beggarly and impoverishing. How they missed their opportunity (Heb. 2:1 ff.).

The revelation of Jahweh in Exodus 34 became the perennial theme of Israel's praises. It unfolds the essential nature of our God in all its moral glory and meaningfulness.

The depth and comprehension of this enunciation of the name Jahweh are unsurpassed in the Old Testament. The three terms for "grace" in the Old Testament, here translated as "merciful," "gracious," and "steadfast love," intensify the gracious character of Jahweh beyond other predicates. The first term (Heb. *rahum*) derives from the word *womb,* which has no plural in Hebrew. When it appears in the plural, it means "loving-kindness," or, more specifically uterine love, the love of a mother for her offspring. It is the tenderness of mother love exercised to one in the closest relationship imaginable. It is a bold concept introducing the sensitivity of the feminine into a relational term, and then using it to express the relationship Jahweh has toward man. The second term (Heb. *hannum)* is derived from the noun form which means the bestowal of kindness that cannot be claimed, the unmerited favor bestowed through the altruisim of a superior apart from any consideration predisposing the action. The final word (Heb. *hesed),* translated "steadfast love," is the loyalty of love and lies at the heart of the covenant idea (1 Sam. 20:8). It may be defined as the oughtness of love, the moral bounden expression of an admitted relationship. It is illustrated in the steadfast love or mercy which the good Samaritan exercised toward the injured Jew. Steadfast love is dilated in the Old Testament as "great" (Ps. 57:11), "abundant" (Ps. 103:8; Ex. 34:6), as "everlasting" (Ps. 100:5), and as "good" (Ps. 63:4). The juxtaposition of these three terms to initiate the disclosure of the name (= nature) of Jahweh creates an emphasis both definitive and unique. A fourth term (Heb. *'emeth)* translated "faithfulness," has the basic idea of firmness. The cognate verb means "to affirm" in the causative tense and "to be confirmed" in the passive. The two verb forms are beautifully joined in a classic passage in Isaiah 7:9: "If you will not *affirm* (that is, *believe*), surely you shall not be *confirmed.*" The play on the two forms of the verb may be further illustrated in two additional translations.

> If you do not confide,
> surely you will not abide.
>
> If you do not have faith,
> surely you will not have staith.

Jahweh is abundant in unchanging fidelity, troth, faithfulness.

To his faithfulness is added the predicate that he is "slow to anger." Anger is a long time coming; he is not easily exasperated. Five terms, then, are the prelude to four verbs thst follow: "keeping," "forgiving," "clearing," "visiting"; they indicate the mode wherewith the verbs will be exercised.

It is unfortunate that most English versions obscure the meaning of "thousands," as though it were for "thousands of individuals." It should be rendered "extending kindness to the thousandth generation" (so NJV) as the parallel in Deuteronomy 5:10 indicates (so ASV mg.). The contrast is between "thousands" and "three" or "four." What thousands of generations are to three or four, that the steadfast love sustains to his wrath. The psalmist phrased it similarly: "His anger is but for a moment, but his favor is for a life time" (Ps. 30:5). The steadfast love is directed to the thousandth generation of those who love Jahweh and keep his commandments. It is not the love, if love it be, that condones; it is the love that flows into the receptive life and elicits the best. The perennial steadfast love assumes the pattern of forgiveness, the "bearing away" of iniquity (aberration from the divine norm), transgression (rebellion against divine authority), and sin (missing the mark). The steadfast love flows in channels of forgiveness, and forgiveness addresses the expansive human problem of estrangement. The major terms for *sin* are here adduced; the vocabulary is essentially represented. In this complex of aberration, rebellion, and failure divine forgiveness brings resolution and renewal, not merely the removal of old obstacles, but the creation of a new relationship.

Nonetheless, there is a governance of steadfast love; it does not bring its mead in license to those who reject Jahweh. Righteousness obtains in the unfortunate areas where men reject Jahweh; judgment visits, else the character of God would be effaced. This steadfast love-judgment visitation theme, it should be noted, is also enunciated in the Decalogue. There it is associated with the "jealousy" of Jahweh. When applied to Jahweh, jealousy means his self-affirmation. At every point of his being, if we may be permitted this expression, Jahweh exercised infinite assertion; otherwise he would be less than God. It suggests that Jahweh is eternally dynamic, and that activity is operative in forgiveness or in judgment at every moment of time and in every situation. It is the moral intensification of the divine dynamic in human history.

There is no need to point out that the disclosure of the divine name in Exodus 34:6–7 assumed a paramount role in the subsequent history of the community of God. Whether recalled in a crisis situation (Num. 14:18), in a penitential national prayer (Neh. 9:17), in a personal lament (Ps. 86:15),[6] or in hymnic praise, the enunciation of Jahweh's name was tremendous; it electrifies us that we have this magnificent God as our ultimate reality.

> He made known his ways to Moses,
> his acts to the people of Israel.
> Jahweh is merciful and gracious,
> slow to anger and abounding in steadfast love.
> He will not always chide,
> nor will he keep his anger for ever.
> He does not deal with us according to our sins,
> nor requite us according to our iniquities.
> For as the heavens are high above the earth,
> so great is his steadfast love toward those who fear him
> (Ps. 103:7–11).

NOTES

[1] Albright, William Foxwell. *From the Stone Age to Christianity.* Baltimore: Johns Hopkins Press, 1940, p. 203.

[2] Westcott, Brooke Foss, *The Epistle to the Hebrews.* London: Macmillan and Co., 1889, pp. 486 f.

[3] There is an underlying thought that the earthly tabernacle was but a replica of the heavenly (Ex. 25:40; Heb. 8:5).

[4] Westcott, *The Epistle to the Hebrews,* p. 286.

[5] Cp. the *Code of Hammurabi* 37, where the contract is cancelled when the tablet is broken.

[6] On this difficult matter see *supra* pp. 16 f.

Selected Bibliography

COMMENTARIES

Cassuto, Umberto. *A Commentary on the Book of Exodus.* Jerusalem: Magnes Press, 1967. Conservative.

Childs, Brevard S. *The Book of Exodus* ("The Old Testament Library") Philadelphia: Westminster Press, 1974. Advanced. Provides a complete and up-to-date bibliography.

Driver, Samuel R. *The Book of Exodus* ("Cambridge Bible for Schools and Colleges"). Cambridge: At the University Press, 1911. Often reprinted. Still the best all around commentary. Critical, devout.

Honeycutt, Roy L., Jr. "Exodus" *(The Broadman Bible Commentary,* Vol. 1). Nashville: Broadman Press, 1969. Popular.

BACKGROUND STUDIES

HISTORICAL

Bright, John. *A History of Israel.* Philadelphia: Westminster Press, 1959. The standard work.

ARCHAEOLOGICAL

Finegan, Jack. *Let My People Go: A Journey Through Exodus.* New York: Harper & Row, 1963.

Montet, Pierre. *Everyday Life in Egypt.* London: Edward Arnold, 1958. The very best in the field.

Pfeiffer, Charles F. *Egypt and the Exodus.* Grand Rapids: Baker Book House, 1964.

Pritchard, James B., ed. *Ancient Near Eastern Texts Relating to the Old Testament.* 3rd ed. Princeton: Princeton University Press, 1969. Indispensable.

EGYPTIAN

Gardiner, Sir Alan. *Egypt of the Pharaohs.* Oxford: At the Clarendon Press, 1971. Masterful.

Wilson, John A. *The Culture of Ancient Egypt.* Chicago: University of Chicago Press, 1951. A splendid work.

THEOLOGICAL AND PRACTICAL

Hebert, Gabriel. *When Israel Came Out of Egypt.* London: SCM Press, 1961. Very suggestive.

Meyer, F. B. *Exodus* ("The R.T.S. Devotional Commentary"). 2 vols. London: Religious Tract Society, n.d. Devotional.

Stock, Augustine. *The Way in the Wilderness: Exodus, Wilderness, and Moses Themes in the Old Testament and New.* Collegeville, Minn.: Liturgical Press, 1969.